US-ISRAELI STRATEGIC COOPERATION IN THE POST-COLD WAR ERA: AN AMERICAN PERSPECTIVE

JCSS Study No. 20

US-ISRAELI STRATEGIC COOPERATION IN THE POST-COLD WAR ERA: AN AMERICAN PERSPECTIVE

Karen L. Puschel

LONDON AND NEW YORK

First published 1992 by Westview Press

Published 2018 by Routledge
52 Vanderbilt Avenue, New York, NY 10017
2 Park Square, Milton Park, Abingdon, Oxon OX14 4RN

Routledge is an imprint of the Taylor & Francis Group, an informa business

Copyright@ 1992 by Tel Aviv University, Jaffee Center for Strategic Studies

All rights reserved. No part of this book may be reprinted or reproduced or utilised in any form or by any electronic, mechanical, or other means, now known or hereafter invented, including photocopying and recording, or in any information storage or retrieval system, without permission in writing from the publishers.

Notice:
Product or corporate names may be trademarks or registered trademarks, and are used only for identification and explanation without intent to infringe.

A CIP catalog record for this book is available from the Library of Congress.

ISBN 13: 978-0-367-21415-9 (hbk)
ISBN 13: 978-0-367-21696-2 (pbk)

The Jaffee Center for Strategic Studies (JCSS)

The Center for Strategic Studies was established at Tel Aviv University at the end of 1977. In 1983 it was named the Jaffee Center for Strategic Studies in honor of Mr. and Mrs. Mel Jaffee. The objective of the Center is to contribute to the expansion of knowledge on strategic subjects and to promote public understanding of and pluralistic thought on matters of national and international security.

The Center relates to the concept of strategy in its broadest meaning, namely, the complex of processes involved in the identification, mobilization and application of resources in peace and war, in order to solidify and strengthen national and international security.

International Board of Trustees

Chairman: Melvin Jaffee
Immediate Past Chairman: Joseph H. Strelitz (deceased)
Robert H. Arnow, Arnold Y. Aronoff, Newton D. Becker, Jack Berlin, Henry Borenstein, Edgar M. Bronfman, Simon Chilewich, Bertram J. Cohn, Stewart M. Colton, Lester Crown, Joseph K. Eichenbaum, Danielle and Shimon Erem, Allan Fainbarg, Dr. Gerald Falwell, Jacob Feldman, Arnold D. Feuerstein, David Furman, Guilford Glazer, Burton E. Glazov, Eugene M. Grant, Vernon Green, Martin J. Gross, Michael M.H. Gross, Irving B. Harris, Betty and Sol Jaffee, Philip M. Klutznick, Judy and Joel Knapp, Fred Kotek, Raymond Kulek, Max L. Kunianski, Mark Lambert, Rose Lederer, Fred W. Lessing, Morris L. Levinson, Edward Levy, Peter A. Magowan, Judd D. Malkin, Hermann Merkin, Stephen Meadow, Monte MonAster, Max Perlman, Milton J. Petrie, Gary P. Ratner, Raphael Recanati, Meshulam Riklis, Morris Rodman, Elihu Rose, Malcolm M. Rosenberg, Irving Schneider, George Shrut, Marvin Simon, Ruth Sinaiko, Ed Stein, Herb Stein, Walter P. Stern, Dr. Robert J. Stoller, Leonard R. Strelitz, James Warren, David Warsaw, Jack D. Weiler, Marvin A. Weiss, Emanuel A. Winston, Bert Wolstein, Paul Yanowicz

CONTENTS

		Page
Acknowledgments		1
Summary		3
Introduction		7
Part I		
Chapter 1.	The Seeds are Planted	11
Chapter 2.	The Reagan Revolution	32
Chapter 3.	The Lebanon Interlude	52
Part II		
Chapter 4.	Strategic Cooperation Becomes Reality	65
Chapter 5.	Strategic Cooperation is Finally Defined	81
Chapter 6.	The Bush Administration	100
Chapter 7.	Storm Clouds Over the Gulf	113
Chapter 8.	Israel Under Attack	127
Part III		
Chapter 9.	Looking to the Future	145
Notes		163
Appendix 1.	Memorandum of Understanding Between the Government of the United States and the Government of Israel on Strategic Cooperation 30 November 1981	178
Appendix 2.	Memorandum of Agreement Between the United States of America and the State of Israel Regarding Joint Political, Security and Economic Cooperation	181
About the Author		184

In memory of my father,
Mendel A. Puschel

Acknowledgments

This study benefited tremendously from the insights of a number of Americans and Israelis involved in the process of strategic cooperation. Interviews with them were, without exception, highly useful and thought-provoking. While several high-level American officials preferred not to speak for attribution, the names of the others follow. My sincere thanks go to all.

On the American side, Ambassador William A. Brown, Colonel James Carney, Alton Frye, Marvin Feuerwerger, Martin Indyk, Ambassador Samuel Lewis, Wayne Limberg, Michael Mandelbaum, Robert Murray, Nicholas Veliotes, William Quandt. On the Israeli side: Dr. Hanan Alon, Hanon Bar-On, Dr. Dore Gold, Dr. Yehuda Ben Meir, Major General (res.) Menachem Meron, MK Yitzhak Rabin, Dr. Barry Rubin, Dr. Elyakim Rubinstein, Major General (res.) Avraham Tamir, and Brigadier General (res.) Mordechai Zippori. I am also indebted to Dr. Vladimir Nosenko and Dr. Sergei Rogov from the Soviet Union and Ambassador Salah Bassiouny and Dr. Ali E. Hillal Dessouki in Cairo, for providing me with their very important perspectives on the issue.

This study could not have been accomplished without the support, advice and stimulation offered by the Jaffee Center for Strategic Studies under the wise leadership of Major General (res.) Aharon Yariv. It was a great privilege to be at the Jaffee Center and to be able to work with and learn from so many exceptional people. I am particularly indebted to Deputy Head of Center Joseph Alpher for his thorough and insightful editing of the study. I wish to thank Brigadier General (res.) Aryeh Shalev, Major General (res.) Shlomo Gazit, Dr. Ariel Levite, Dr. Efraim Kam and Prof. Aharon Klieman for their thoughtful suggestions and comments on the first draft of this work. And I am most grateful for the support and friendship offered by the administrative staff of the Jaffee Center, particularly by Moshe Grundman, Tova Polonsky, Shulamit Reich, Alexandra Szilvassy and Gal Levi.

Funding for this research came from the United States Institute of Peace; I am grateful for the Institute's support throughout the process. The opinions, findings and conclusions or recommendations expressed in this publication are those of the author and do not necessarily reflect the views of the United States Institute of Peace. Nor do the views expressed in this study necessarily reflect those of the US Department of State or any other US or Israeli agency or institution. I wish also to thank the United States Information Agency at the American Embassy in Tel Aviv for the use of its excellent library facilities.

Finally, a special note of appreciation to my husband, Jack Segal, who should be credited with coming up with the idea of the study, and who throughout the sometimes painful process of research and writing was unfailingly supportive and encouraging.

Karen Puschel
Washington, December 1991

Summary

The passing of the Cold War and the development of a cooperative and even friendly relationship between the United States and the Soviet Union/Russia have transformed American foreign policy in two key areas. The first is in the system of security alliances established by the US after World War II to protect what it considered to be its vital interests around the globe. Today, as a result of the reduced threat posed by Russia to countries outside its borders, longstanding security alliances developed by the United States in Europe and the Far East have lost their core raison d'etre and are now changing indelibly.

The second area altered by the end of the Cold War is the American approach to regional disputes around the globe. At the core of US involvement in Korea and Vietnam, and more recently in Pakistan and Afghanistan, was the belief that because the Soviets were involved, the US had to be as well. Now, with the ending of Soviet military aid to Afghanistan, the withdrawal of military forces from Cuba, and the pullout of the Soviet presence in Vietnam, America has had to consider for the first time what its real interests are in these regions. Support for military aid to Pakistan, which used to receive the third largest disbursement of US aid after Israel and Egypt, has already dropped significantly.

This study examines the effects of the passing of the Cold War on one important area of US foreign policy: the strategic relationship between the United States and Israel, termed "strategic cooperation" since 1983. US policy toward Israel since its conception in 1948 has been, as this study will relate, greatly shaped by the American drive to contain Soviet influence in the Middle East. Moreover, the very concept, born in the 1980s, of Israel as a "strategic ally" of the United States, came from a shared sense of alliance between the US and Israel against the Soviet Union and its proxies in the Middle East. One would thus expect US-Israeli strategic cooperation to be buffeted by the twin pressures outlined above concerning US alliance structures and American regional policies in the post-Cold War era.

But in fact, this study concludes that US-Israeli strategic cooperation is not likely to be significantly eroded by the fading of the Cold War. Despite the emphasis in public on the Soviet threat as the basis for strategic cooperation, the decision to initiate the program in late 1983 reflected a broad variety of concerns on the American side; countering Soviet influence played a relatively minor role. Moreover, with the actual implementation of strategic cooperation from 1984 on, reliance on the Soviet threat diminished even further as both sides turned their attention to finding areas of practical cooperation that were of mutual benefit.

Today, the institutionalization of that process helps to ensure its continued success. Even more important, strategic cooperation is now widely viewed as an essential element of the US commitment to Israel's security. Thus, even if the US wishes to go back, this would be at the risk of undermining deterrence in the region and, thereby, strategic stability as well. Moreover, the American-Israeli strategic cooperation program has proved much less upsetting to the Arabs than once predicted. Hence it seems to be here to stay.

But if the overall fact of strategic cooperation is no longer at issue today, the nature and scope of the relationship is subject to change as a result of largely indirect effects from the passing of the Cold War. First, one of the main aspects of strategic cooperation from Israel's point of view — military assistance — seems unlikely to increase significantly given the post-Cold War emphasis on fiscal restraint in the United States. Particularly as the US military copes with a huge budget reduction over the next five years, there is likely to be growing pressure from the services to cut back on the number of joint exercises with Israel and possibly even the number of ship visits to Haifa Port.

Moreover, no compelling political rationale exists today for expanding strategic cooperation. In the past, strategic relations between the US and Israel tended to grow either as a result of progress on the peace front, which then led to increased US commitments to Israel, or as a result of US frustration with the Arab states — which led Washington to focus even more on Israel as the only reliable venue for American influence in the region.

Today, neither of these conditions exists. The US is in the enviable position of being the only superpower in the region and has many new options vis-a-vis the Arab states. And while peace would indisputably lead to a further increase in strategic cooperation, the actual peace process seems likely to put additional strain on the relationship. Indeed, from the US perspective, strategic cooperation has never simply been about creating military possibilities in the region, but about developing an overall environment of security for Israel that would help to create possibilities for peace — both through deterrence and through Israel's willingness to engage in an active peace process. This subtle linkage between peace and strategic cooperation constitutes one of the most important differences between the way the United States views strategic cooperation, and Israel's conception.

Some Americans and Israelis have long asserted that Israel's importance to the United States lies in its ability to assist Washington directly in the latter's military policies vis-a-vis the Soviet Union or in the region itself. If this is indeed the case, then strategic cooperation today is in trouble. Not only is the Soviet scenario gone, but the Persian Gulf War underscored that, as far as America is concerned, Israel's status remains too problematic to warrant relying on it in a regional crisis.

Yet this study found that the US never entered into the program of strategic cooperation with the idea of relying on Israel's military might in the region. Rather, there was the hope that a strong and confident Israel would be more willing to takes risks for peace. There were also pressures that stemmed from domestic politics at home. Finally, there was the unalterable fact of Israel's strength in the region and the special friendship between the two countries which, over the years, had created an increasingly firm commitment to Israel's security by the United States.

Today, it is this complex mix of motivations for strategic cooperation that serves as its greatest protection. Because there was no one imperative for strategic cooperation, there will likely never be a single catalyst for its decline. Strategic cooperation exists, in the final analysis, because of an extremely close US-Israeli relationship that is committed to ensuring the security of the Israeli people. This in turn rests on American identification and sympathy with the nation of Israel for historical, moral and political reasons.

Introduction

The world has undergone tremendous change since Mikhail Gorbachev came to power in the Soviet Union in 1985. From the toppling of the Berlin Wall and the breakup of the Warsaw Pact to the disintegration of the Union of Soviet Socialist Republics itself, events have proved a catalyst for fast-moving changes around the globe, the implications of which we are just beginning to understand.

Nowhere are these implications more far-reaching than with regard to the system of security alliances established by the US around the world. Already security structures in Europe and the Far East are indelibly changing. Over time, it is not at all certain that longstanding alliances such as NATO will even remain.

One place where the Soviet threat has played an instrumental role in the formation of US policies is the State of Israel. While humanitarian sympathies and identification with Israel's democratic and moral values have provided a steady basis of support for Israel since its foundation, US policy toward Israel has more often than not been affected by Washington's drive to contain Soviet influence in the Middle East. Only in the last 10 years has it become common to refer to Israel as a "strategic ally" of the United States; that usage reflected a shared sense of alliance against the Soviet Union and its proxies in the Middle East.

But now the Cold War is over and US policymakers are no longer preoccupied with the specter of a Soviet threat to the region, or the possibility that events in the Middle East could lead to a superpower clash. While Russia is not out of the picture — its weapons continue to be provided to the region and Moscow remains diplomatically active — from the American perspective Moscow is no longer the enemy but, increasingly, a possible ally in the Middle East.

This study examines the effects of the passing of the Cold War on one important aspect of US policy toward Israel: the complex and wide-ranging web of relationships between the two countries captured by the term "strategic cooperation." There has long been much mystery and difference of opinion as to the meaning of strategic cooperation for either the United States or Israel. While one school of thought has maintained that strategic cooperation evolved as a direct consequence of Israel's growing importance to the US, including against the Soviets, another perspective holds that strategic cooperation is simply a reflection of American domestic politics at work.

Which perspective comes closer to the truth? The answer is important for any attempt to understand where US-Israeli strategic relations may be headed in the future. At issue are not only US security policies in the region and toward the USSR, but also the complex inter-relationship linking Israel's security and the search for Middle East peace.

This study addresses the issue in three parts. The first examines why and how strategic cooperation came to be established, starting with the conceptual backdrop of the 1970s and exploring in greater detail the codification of strategic cooperation during the Reagan years. The second section examines how strategic cooperation was implemented, beginning in 1984. The final section explores the legacy of strategic cooperation for the future, including the effects of the changed US-Soviet relationship as well as the aftermath of the war in the Gulf. One key issue followed throughout the study is the importance of the Soviet threat for the making of US policy in this area, vis-a-vis the relative importance of other motivations for strategic cooperation, including the role of domestic politics and the importance of the US search for peace.

One important note on definitions. For purposes of this paper, the author uses "strategic cooperation" in two ways: one refers to the formal program that was agreed to by both sides in November 1983, and which provides an overall framework for everything from US aid to Israel to prepositioning of equipment in Israel. The second, broader usage refers to the way in which Americans and Israelis have come to perceive the strategic relationship over the years. Judging by its history, strategic cooperation cannot simply be described as a military program. Rather, it is a complex web of political-military activities that touch the very heart of the US-Israeli relationship.

Part I

Chapter 1. The Seeds are Planted

Early Attitudes and Perceptions

When the United States cast its vote in 1948 in support of the establishment of the State of Israel, neither Harry Truman nor any other key foreign policy figure in Washington believed that the tiny state would be of assistance in furthering American strategic objectives. Indeed, opposition to Israel from within the foreign policy community was intense. It was largely based on the belief that US support for Israel would be harmful to key US strategic and political interests in the region — particularly, preserving western access to oil, maintaining friendly relations with the Arab world, and countering the spread of communism.[1]

Concern about communism had taken on increasing urgency and importance for the United States as the tenuous wartime alliance with the Soviet Union gave way to hostility. The Korean War, the end of Stalinism, and the rise of a new communist menace on the Chinese mainland led Washington to fear the spread of Soviet and communist influence both at home and abroad. The Middle East with its vital resources, located practically in the Soviet Union's backyard, was one area of concern.

President Eisenhower in particular was inclined to view the Middle East as a subset of the larger Soviet threat facing the United States. During his eight years in office, a key preoccupation was to build an anti-Soviet alliance with other states in the region. Far from being seen as an important state to woo, Israel was seen primarily as a problem. Asked in 1954 about granting military aid to the Israelis, Eisenhower responded that, "We are not rendering anyone assistance to start a war or to indulge in a conflict with others of our friends. When we give military assistance, that is for the common purpose of opposing communism."[2] From Eisenhower's perspective, Israel was not part of the struggle against communism and was even potentially dangerous to American "friends" in the region.

Not only was a strategic rationale missing for improved relations with Israel during this period, there was also little domestic pressure on the administration to this end. Peter Grose notes that

Israel faded from America's public agenda in the early 1950s and that Eisenhower was able to address even Jewish audiences during this period "without once mentioning the State of Israel."[3] Steven Spiegel also notes that, perhaps because Israel was not facing any immediate threat to its existence, Jewish lobbying efforts in America were directed elsewhere.[4]

The net result was that, despite the critical diplomatic support given to Israel at its formation, the US was unwilling to be perceived as working with Israel, let alone as allied with it. Rather, just as Truman had been swayed by humanitarian concerns in 1948 to support Israel, so too was the general American view of Israel shaped by moral and religious underpinnings and an appreciation for the common cultural, political and ideological ties between the two nations. The 1952 Republican Party platform referred to a "friendly interest" in Israel which appealed to "our deepest humanitarian instincts."[5] This attitude was reflected in US aid policies at the time: while there was support for economic aid based on a principled commitment to Israel, such aid was controversial, hotly debated, and carefully balanced by similar aid for Arab states. Military aid to Israel was out of the question.

The one area where appreciation did exist for Israel was in the intelligence field. Here Israel could be seen as an asset, not just a liability, vis-a-vis the Soviet threat, and US intelligence officials were interested in Israel's access to and connections in the Eastern Bloc. The first copy of Khrushchev's secret speech denouncing Stalin reportedly arrived in the US via an Israeli source. What with the number of new emigres in Israel, the Eastern Bloc arms obtained by Israel in the late 1940s, and the combat experience against Soviet equipment gained during the Independence and Suez wars, Israel had much to offer the American intelligence effort against the Soviets.

The Winds of Change

The largely negative official American view of Israel gradually began to change both in response to domestic politics within the United States and to developments in the Middle East. In 1956, even as the Eisenhower Administration cut back economic aid to

Israel and turned down any request for military aid, the Democratic Party pledged to redress the arms imbalance in the area by "selling or supplying defensive weapons to Israel, and will take such steps, including security guarantees, as may be required to deter aggression and war in the area."[6] When Democratic candidate John F. Kennedy won the 1960 presidential election on the narrowest of margins and with over 80 percent of the Jewish vote, it seemed clear that, at least in the White House, Israel would be given a more sympathetic hearing.

And, indeed, both rhetorical support for Israel and practical support in the form of weapons supply, changed significantly under President Kennedy and then President Johnson. Both men embraced Israel as a positive force consistent with American ideals and underscored, in vague terms, the US commitment to Israel's security. In 1962 Israel received its first major weapons system from the United States when President Kennedy agreed to deliver HAWK anti-aircraft missiles. This was followed by the provision of $80 million in tanks, first through the FRG and then directly from the US. In February 1966, in what was a significant turning point, President Johnson agreed to sell 48 Skyhawk bombers to Israel.[7]

These changes should not, however, be seen as simply the result of a more sympathetic political setting in Washington. Even more important were the changes that were taking place in the Middle East region itself. These argued for a new US approach toward growing Soviet influence and Arab radicalism there. The Eisenhower years, despite the tough approach to Israel, had not resulted in an enhanced American position in the Arab world or in blocking Soviet advances. By the 1960s increasing amounts of Soviet arms were being provided to the region, leading to concern in Washington that the regional balance of power could tip toward the radical Arabs. It was this perceived need to find a counterbalance that provided the key impulse for the US to change its longstanding policy against providing arms to Israel.

However, in many important respects this change in policy fell short of what Israeli leaders saw as necessary or desirable for Israel's security. David Ben-Gurion, Israel's first prime minister, had tried to no avail to secure Israel's strategic position through an alliance with the United States or NATO in the 1950s and 1960s. Despite a more sympathetic attitude toward Israel in the 1960s on the part of key individuals in Washington, it does not appear that the idea was seriously considered even then. Indeed, in the Kennedy-Johnson years, Washington remained concerned that any closer alliance with Israel would be at the expense of more strategically important American interests in the Arab world. Moreover, American preoccupation with Vietnam meant that there was little interest in courting further entanglements overseas.

The Six-Day War — a Watershed

The sweeping victory by Israeli forces during the Six-Day War in 1967 was a watershed in the evolving US-Israeli relationship. On the eve of war, US policy continued to be marked by hesitancy and a certain degree of ambivalence. The Johnson Administration deemed illegal Nasser's closure of the Straits of Tiran to Israel's shipping and sought, in the days leading up to war, a solution that would protect Israeli rights. But both President Johnson and the Congress were concerned that the US not become involved in another war. Israel's request before the war for guarantees from the US went unanswered.[8] And, once war began, Washington neither explicitly supported nor criticized Israel.

But by the end of the war, the powerful demonstration of force by Israel had completely altered strategic calculations in the region. US concern about being saddled with responsibility for a "loser" in the Middle East was alleviated. Not only could Israel clearly take care of itself, but it emerged from the war in a strong position to effect other events in the region. It is doubtful whether the closer US-Israeli relationship that developed thereafter would have occurred without this striking victory by Israeli forces.

The war also deeply affected the domestic situation within the United States; practically overnight, there was a tremendous surge of identification with the Israeli state. Immigration to Israel from the United States went up dramatically, as did the level of interest toward Israel within the United States.[9] All in all, support for Israel grew to some four to five times greater than support for Arabs — a substantially higher margin than before the war.[10] This not only gave an important boost to pro-Israel lobbying efforts, it created a political environment that was highly sympathetic to support for Israel.

This would have very important ramifications just a year later when the administration considered increased arms for Israel, specifically the sale of sophisticated F-4 Phantom jets. Though faced with widespread opposition to providing Israel with these combat aircraft on the part of the foreign policy bureaucracy in Washington, every presidential candidate would come out in favor of the sale, as would both the Republican and Democratic parties.[11] Underscoring the growing politicization of the issue, Congress eventually added an amendment to the foreign aid bill pressing the president to sell the aircraft to Israel.[12]

Although no such dramatic swing in views occurred in the foreign policy institutions charged with conducting US policy in the region, even here the war ushered in a greater awareness of the positive possibilities that could result from cooperation with Israel. One immediate area of interest was once again intelligence, particularly that pertaining to the Soviet Union. The intelligence relationship between the two countries became formalized for the first time during this period, reflecting the greater legitimacy that US-Israel relations had assumed.

In particular, cooperation expanded significantly because of Israel's combat experience dealing with Soviet weaponry and military doctrine. Israel had just emerged from a successful war fought against Soviet-supplied Arab states. Just 18 months later it would be involved in a protracted conflict with Egypt (the War of Attrition) which, in many ways, became a major proving ground for the military equipment of the two superpowers. One important example: the Soviet anti-aircraft system defending Egypt proved vulnerable to western-type combat aircraft flown by Israeli pilots.[13] From the perspective of American military planners preoccupied with the Soviet threat, Israel had become a laboratory for developing countermeasures to Soviet weaponry and tactics.

But perhaps the most important effect of the newly demonstrated Israeli strength was in the area of US regional strategy. While the State Department tended to see the Israeli conquest of Arab territory as creating yet another problem for US policy, key individuals began to recognize that peace could not be based on a weak Israel, but rather on a balance of power in the region.

Moreover, given the growth of Soviet influence there, the radicalization of Arab politics, and the need to shoulder an ever-increasing burden of responsibility for the Middle East in the wake of the British pull-out, the United States was in need of new assets in the region. Practically overnight, Israel's demonstrated military strength significantly improved American leverage in the Middle East.

So it was that by the time of Richard Nixon's election as president in 1968 and his appointment of Henry Kissinger as National Security Advisor, the key pieces were in place for a new phase in the US-Israeli relationship. It would be founded principally on the common goal of countering the Soviets, and backed up by a domestic constituency largely sympathetic toward Israel. Arms supplies would be a key expression of the new US approach. Establishing a principle that continues to this day, candidate Richard Nixon stated that Israel needed a "technological military margin to more than offset her hostile neighbors' numerical superiority."[14] While implementation of this policy would be neither smooth nor easy, domestic political support for Israel would ensure that it became an established aspect of US policy.[15]

Thwarting the Soviets

By the beginning of the 1970s, Soviet influence was growing throughout the Middle East, most importantly in Egypt. In the early months of 1970, 15,000 Soviet troops arrived in Egypt, operating some 150 aircraft and manning an extensive surface-to-air missile complex. The Soviets even participated in the War of Attrition between Egypt and Israel, as became clear when Israel shot down five Soviet-piloted MiGs in the summer of 1970. Moscow's direct involvement added a new dimension to the Arab-Israel conflict and unquestionably had a tremendous effect on Washington's perception of events in the Middle East.

Indeed, more than even President Eisenhower, Nixon's foreign policy in the Middle East would be motivated by the desire to drive the Soviets out or at least balance the significant gains that Moscow had made in the region. Since Soviet influence rested primarily on Moscow's military relationship with radical Arab states, an essential element of Nixon and Kissinger's strategy would be to demonstrate that the Soviets could not bring the Arab world what it sought: the defeat of Israel and the regaining of territory lost to it during the Six-Day War. Flowing from this strategy was the need for a closer US-Israeli relationship, both to send the message to the Arabs that Israel's strength was uncompromising, and to establish the basis for one day "bringing" Israel to the negotiating table.

Yet Washington did not move to embrace Israel as a strategic partner. Traditional skepticism about Israel continued to be strong in key institutions, such as the State Department, that saw Israel's strength and regional policies as simply making the diplomat's job that much tougher. As Kissinger notes in his memoirs, his belief that the primary US objective must first be to confront the growing Soviet presence in the region was definitely a minority view. "Most in the government" blamed Israel for the deteriorating conditions in the Middle East and were opposed to any new military assistance for Israel, which Kissinger saw as a crucial part of his broader strategy.[16]

Moreover, it is important to realize that even Nixon and Kissinger's appreciation of Israel's value was in the context of their strategic objectives at any given time: countering the Soviets, wooing the Arabs, and maintaining Israel's security. The decade of the 1970s would show just how different Israel's value could be perceived, depending on which of these strategic objectives was in the ascendancy.

The stage was thus set for events during the 1970s which would leave an indelible legacy for strategic cooperation. At three distinct junctures the nature of the US-Israeli relationship — including the nature of the role that Israel could play on behalf of US interests — would be tested and redefined. At the time, none of this was ever called strategic cooperation. Yet these were the beginnings of the conceptual process and debate from which the formal strategic cooperation program would eventually grow.

The "Golden Years" of Cooperation

In 1970, an event occurred that was tailor-made for testing the tentative new US-Israeli relationship, since it involved the intertwining of regional and superpower interests. In September of that year, King Hussein of Jordan found himself in fierce battle with Palestinians intent on toppling his regime. As the situation deteriorated, a Syrian tank division crossed into Jordan and advanced toward the northern Jordanian city of Irbid.

For Israel, the fall of the King might have resulted in the creation of a radical Palestinian state on its border and the clear strengthening of one its most dangerous foes, Syria. For the United States, the situation risked nothing less than a possible change in the strategic balance of power in the region. Syria and the PLO were clients of Moscow; with the Soviets already deeply involved in Egypt, a further success in Jordan could have sealed the fate of the entire region.

There was thus a convergence of interests between the US and Israel in favor of blocking the threat to the Hashemite Kingdom. What made this situation truly exceptional was that Israel was called upon to use its military superiority against that threat.

According to Yitzhak Rabin, then-Israeli ambassador in Washington, King Hussein asked Israel, through the US, to use its air force against the Syrian forces in northern Jordan.[17] Kissinger recounts that the decision to rely on Israeli forces was not an easy one for Washington (until late in the crisis President Nixon preferred to rely only on US action, not Israeli), but that eventually the US decided that employing its own forces might appear too provocative to Moscow and thus too risky.[18]

Meanwhile, with the specter of potential Soviet involvement not far off, Israel demanded — and received — a US commitment to assist it in the event of a Soviet countermove. Thus a clear division of roles was effected: the US deployed a large naval contingent just off the coast of Lebanon which eventually included two aircraft carriers, 18 destroyers, and a Marine landing team. With other forces assigned as backup, Washington was ready, according to Kissinger, to evacuate Americans should it prove necessary, and to deter Soviet intervention against Israel.[19]

Israel's role was to respond militarily to the Syrian move (and conceivably even an Iraqi move) inside Jordan. To that end, Israel drew up plans that included the possibility of both air and ground attacks (despite King Hussein's request for air strikes alone) and began to reinforce its troops in the Golan.[20] In the end, the US augmentation of its forces and the Israeli buildup provided the needed boost for King Hussein to turn the situation around. The Syrian forces withdrew and the Palestinians were defeated by Jordanian forces in what became known in Palestinian circles as "Black September."

The incident stood as a clear example of US-Israeli partnership in the region or, as Yitzhak Rabin would later term it, "strategic cooperation in action."[21] At the height of the conflict, there were numerous exchanges between the two governments on Israeli military planning and even a few examples of tactical cooperation between Sixth Fleet forces and Israel.[22] The net effect was to highlight Israel's deterrent value in the region and to challenge the longstanding proposition that Israel was no more than a liability to US interests in the region.

Shortly after the crisis, the president sent a message of appreciation to Israel which stated that the US was "fortunate in having an ally like Israel in the Middle East."[23] It was the first such official reference to Israel as an "ally." Meanwhile, in the first of a long series of requests for significant military aid for Israel, President Nixon asked to provide it with $500 million in military credits.

Yet the US umbrella, reluctantly given, was also withdrawn in the wake of the conflict. Hence the president's message also stated that "all aspects of the exchanges between us" were no longer applicable and that, should a new situation arise, fresh exchanges would be necessary.[24] Still, as observers would note, "if the US could undertake joint military planning with Israel, a country with which the US had no formal defense pact, even to the point of promising an 'umbrella' of US protection against any Soviet move against Israel, then such a binding arrangement could be repeated."[25]

The combined effect of direct Soviet involvement in the region, US-Israeli cooperation starting with the War of Attrition, and the joint effort to save the Jordanian monarchy would create what some Israelis have termed the "golden age" of US-Israeli strategic relations.[26] Writing almost 10 years later, Rabin noted that he still looked back on the US message of appreciation with nostalgia, seeing it as the most far-reaching statement ever made by an American president on the mutuality of the alliance between the two countries.[27]

Not only was there an unusually close degree of coordination between the two sides, there was a perceived sense of "equality" that has not been matched since. Israel was not yet heavily dependent on US aid; and US interest in Israel was not simply based on moral grounds or domestic pressures, but on national interests. As Abba Eban would comment, "While Truman and Johnson had strong sentiments toward Israel, with Nixon it was just a matter of interests."[28]

The effect of the incident on Washington's thinking was mixed. As Spiegel has noted, Nixon and Kissinger's major goal remained to thwart Soviet objectives in the area and not to befriend Israel.[29] The foreign policy bureaucracy saw the incident as a diversion from the key goal of achieving an Arab-Israeli settlement; some would even question whether the King had ever really been in mortal danger. But from the point of view of Israel's evolving relationship with the United States, the Jordan crisis stood as a clear example of the way strategic cooperation between the US and Israel could positively affect events in the region.

The 1973 War

If US-Israeli cooperation in saving the Hashemite Kingdom stood as one form of strategic cooperation, events just three years later would testify to a very different aspect: defense of the Israeli state. During the Yom Kippur War, in which Syrian and Egyptian forces launched a surprise attack on Israel, the US for the first time openly and dramatically assisted Israel against its Arab neighbors.

While one former US ambassador to Israel, Sam Lewis, termed the US-Israeli wartime effort "strategic cooperation of the highest order,"[30] in fact the set of motivations on the American side were more complex than the simple desire to follow through on the longstanding US commitment to Israel's security.

On the one hand, an historical and moral commitment to the State of Israel had been displayed by the United States since 1948, and had been greatly enhanced with the groundswell of popular support for Israel following the 1967 war. Spiegel notes that the Yom Kippur War was the first Middle East conflict in which domestic support for Israel — especially arms resupplies — was pronounced, unified and vocal.[31] Kissinger indicated as much when he declared shortly after the war, "It has been a constant American policy supported in every Administration and carrying wide bipartisan support that the existence of Israel will be supported by the United States. This has been our policy in the absence of any formal arrangements and it has never been challenged no matter which Administration was in office."[32]

But as with many things, the situation in 1973 was not unequivocal: it became clear that the US had no ready prescriptions for a situation in which Israel was under attack but not perceived to be in "real danger." Under these conditions, two other American objectives weighed more heavily: to avoid a superpower confrontation even while ensuring that Moscow did not walk away from the conflict with its influence and prestige enhanced; and to minimize the damage to US-Arab relations, even possibly setting the stage for a significant improvement of US relations with the Arab world after the war.

For the first week of war, American experts believed that Israel would quickly and easily turn the tables on its Arab attackers; consequently, Washington was primarily concerned with minimizing the effects of another crushing Israeli victory on the Arabs. It is noteworthy that at no point during the crisis, despite the clear attack on Israel, did the US make references to Arab "aggression."[33] Moreover, the overall American posture early in the war might best be described as "low-profile." For instance, the US was reluctant for its own military aircraft to be seen flying into Tel Aviv.

It was only as it became clear that Israel was in difficulty that Washington gradually began to respond. But even here there were complicating factors, for at the same time Soviet activity greatly escalated, including the beginning of an airlift of weapons to the

Arab states. Indeed, the two most dramatic examples of US activity on behalf of Israel both appeared to have been taken with an eye toward Moscow. Three days after the beginning of the Soviets' airlift to their Arab clients, the US began its own massive airlift, one of the largest resupply efforts ever carried out. The second dramatic US action taken during the war — the decision to increase the state of readiness of US forces — also came in response to Soviet action, in this case a threat to send Soviet combat units into the region.[34]

Thus it becomes difficult to sort out whether the US came to Israel's aid because of its longstanding support for Israel (and because of domestic political pressures) or because of strategic considerations related to countering the USSR. The 1973 war underscored how inseparable the two interests had become. From Nixon and Kissinger's viewpoint, *because* of US identification with Israel, the defeat of Israel at the hands of Soviet-backed clients would have constituted a geopolitical disaster.[35] Hence their immediate concerns were probably fed by strategic calculations; America's moral commitment to Israel, however, was a key domestic political factor defining their parameters for action.

Regardless of why the US ended up assisting Israel so dramatically, the effect was another watershed in the US-Israeli relationship. The very fact of US support for Israel created an important precedent in the relationship and helped further to refine the US commitment to Israel. In the first instance, overwhelming sympathy in Congress for aid to Israel led Nixon to request $2.2 billion in arms authorization, $1.5 billion of which would be provided, at Congress' insistence, in grants to Israel.[36] This unprecedented level of assistance in turn led to a new phase in US-Israeli defense relations.

Yet compared with the status of the relationship three years earlier, the halcyon days of cooperation, at least from Israel's perspective, seemed to be over. While the US had emerged from the war even more committed to Israel's security, many American officials now tended to see this as a largely one-sided relationship because of Israel's growing dependence on US aid and its need for US assistance during the war itself.[37] Indeed, even as both candidates in their 1976 presidential campaign promised increased assistance to Israel, some elements of the foreign policy bureaucracy became even more outspoken in their criticism of Israel.[38]

Israel's role in US strategy also changed following the war, as Kissinger moved into "phase two" of his plan for expelling the Soviets from the region and improving American ties with the Arab world. From the beginning of the war, Kissinger did not hide the fact that one of his primary objectives was to create a postwar environment conducive for launching a viable peace process. The strategy of the previous years of shutting Moscow out of the region had begun to bear fruit in 1972 when Soviet troops were expelled from Egypt. The war generated tremendous pressure on the US to resolve the Arab-Israel conflict and so take advantage of new opportunities to improve its position in the Arab world.

As long as American policy was designed primarily to frustrate Arab reliance on Soviet support, American and Israeli policies had been practically identical. But now Israel was being asked to play a role that had as one of its objectives the improvement of the American position in the Arab world. While from Washington's perspective this was still part of a grand strategy in which Israel was the pivotal player, from Israel's standpoint the premise of its role had been turned upside down. No longer was Israel being valued for its strength and its ability to affect events in the region. Rather, its value now stemmed from its willingness to compromise some of that strength.[39]

Meanwhile Israel had drawn some of its own lessons from the war. While it recognized and appreciated the American contribution to the war and the importance of US weaponry for its security, it also was uncomfortable with the "unequal" nature of the wartime partnership. Moreover, the war had also demonstrated the "price" of a closer relationship with the United States. There was a lingering perception that had the US not repeatedly warned Israel that it must not initiate war, Israel would not have been in such a weak position in the first week of the conflict. Moreover, the fact that the war ended tactically victorious for Israel but strategically inconclusive was seen as a result of American pressures that reflected interests not necessarily identical with Israel's.[40]

One subtle effect of the war and the subsequent increase in US military aid was a growing Israeli effort to articulate the many ways that Israel contributed to US interests. One of the first such attempts was made by Deputy Premier and Foreign Minister Yigal Allon in December 1974. Allon stated that Israel's existence was of "essential interest" to the United States because of the role that Israel played in maintaining stability in a volatile area.[41] In an interview less than a year later, Allon went further, terming Israel an American asset that did not work against US relations in the Arab world, and referring to the joint interests that bound the two countries.[42]

By the time Menachem Begin became prime minister, this approach had evolved into a full-fledged campaign for US recognition of Israel's strategic value. President Carter recalled that during a visit by Begin in early 1979, the prime minister "did not seem particularly interested in the terms of the peace talks. His purpose seemed to be to convince us that Israel should be the dominant power in the area, and that it was our only reliable ally in the Middle East."[43] To this end, according to Carter, Begin recalled Israel's help in 1970 and noted Israel's willingness to join Egypt in an attack on Libya or to defend Saudi Arabia. While part of Begin's intensity was clearly the result of his own personal experiences and his skepticism of any support based on moral reasons alone, his effort to establish Israel's value for the United States also was aimed at dispelling the notion of a one-sided partnership that had emerged after 1973, and thereby justifying the huge sums of US aid going to Israel.

A Question of Peace

Peace efforts would dominate US policy in the region for the rest of the decade. Preoccupation with the Soviet Union had diminished with the onset of detente and setbacks to the Soviet position in the Middle East. This in turn created new opportunities for the US in the Arab world which Washington was eager to exploit. The key to enjoying good relations with both the Arab states and Israel was for the United States to find an Arab-Israeli accommodation. This process, which saw interim successes involving both Israel and

Egypt as well as Israel and Syria, culminated in 1979 with the signing of the Israeli-Egyptian Peace Treaty.

In one sense, the peace process can be seen as yet another example of strategic cooperation between the US and Israel. It clearly involved strategic interests of both sides as well as cooperation. Even if the US and Israel disagreed over specific aspects of the negotiations, there was a common strategic interest in the possibility of peace that bound the two sides together. Moreover, the US-Israeli relationship was fundamental to the peace process itself, both because of the US role as facilitator and because it was largely the strength of US-Israel relations that provided Washington with its diplomatic cards.

From a different perspective, the peace process came to be viewed as the antithesis of strategic cooperation because it seemed to suggest that, after peace, Israel had no other role to play on behalf of US interests in the region. Admittedly, US preoccupation with the Soviets had diminished following the 1973 war. But even when the Soviet threat loomed large again following the 1979 Soviet invasion of Afghanistan and the revolution in Iran that threatened to destabilize the region, still Washington resisted the notion that Israel could assist the US in its military-strategic objectives in the region.[4] This denial that Israel had any significant strategic value for the US except in the realm of cooperating toward peace did not go down well with the Begin government. It was looking for a more affirmative statement of Israel's worth to the United States.

Meanwhile, the advent of the Carter Administration produced a resurgence of the view that the primary reasons for the American commitment to Israel were historical, moral, religious, cultural, and democratic. Not that the US was any less committed to Israel; there could be no doubt that President Carter was firmly committed to Israel's security and believed intensely that a secure Israel was a requisite to peace. Nor did the reemphasis on the US moral commitment mean that the bilateral relationship was doomed to perpetual "inequality." From Carter's perspective, there was a natural equality between the two countries that flowed from the mutual respect and longstanding relations. Early on in his tenure, clearly recognizing Israeli sensitivity over the appearance of a one-sided relationship, the president made his views clear on this issue: "Many people in our country have looked on our relationship with Israel as one of support and one of friendship that was to Israel's benefit. I have never looked on it that way. I consider it to be an equal partnership that has derived, for our country and for the cause of freedom, tremendous benefits for us."[45]

But Carter did not see a grander role for Israel in US policy. In the first years of his term, there was no perceived requirement for help from Israel. By the end of his term, when there was a need for a stronger American military posture in the region, Carter was so frustrated with the Israeli government led by Menachem Begin that the idea of a strategic partnership seemed out of the question.

Thus it is perhaps all the more ironic that President Carter's success on the peace front would help to spur strategic cooperation in the 1980s Whatever else might be said, the Israeli-Egyptian Peace Treaty stood as the first key example of how the US could indeed have close relations with both the Arab world and the Jewish state. It thus helped to legitimize closer and more explicit cooperation with Israel.

Moreover, the very process of achieving peace led to a significant expansion of the US commitment to Israel and of ties between the two countries, including in the defense field. Unintentionally, the spinoff effects of the peace process would create a web of interests and connections between Jerusalem and Washington that would define future parameters for US decisionmakers. Even if Carter resisted the idea that Israel had a strategic role besides peace, by the advent of the Reagan Administration it would seem silly to many people not to rely on Israel — given increasing American aid to it, the growing US commitment to Israel, and Israel's demonstrated willingness to cooperate with the US in the defense realm.

For instance, the same day the interim agreement between Israel and Egypt was signed in 1975, the US and Israel signed three other documents on political, energy and defense issues.[46] What would be most remembered was a US pledge not to talk with the PLO and to coordinate in advance any political moves or initiatives regarding the Middle East. Yet there were also several significant

elements for the burgeoning US-Israeli defense relationship:
— A US pledge to be responsive on a long-term basis to Israel's defense needs and a commitment to supply advanced types of equipment, such as the F-16 combat aircraft;
— a statement of the gravity with which the United States would view any threat to Israel's security from a "world power," i.e., the Soviet Union;
— and a commitment to conclude contingency planning for military resupply of Israel in a crisis.

Four years later, the Camp David Accords would bring about even more explicit commitments from the US regarding issues relating to Israel's security.[47] Of the greatest practical significance, the US agreed to provide up to $3 billion for construction of two airbases in the Negev and to assist in meeting other relocation costs or equipment purchases as the sides might agree. This, in addition to already established annual aid levels, would lead to a massive collaborative project involving the defense establishments of both countries.

Another breakthrough that would have significant long-term effects, particularly for the Israeli military, was a Memorandum of Agreement on defense cooperation signed in 1979. The agreement ushered in increased cooperative research and development by the two sides, and opened the way for Israeli military exports to the United States. Over the years, such cooperation would become an important element of Israel's effort to maintain an independent military-industrial capacity both in research and development and in production, despite the small size of its own internal defense market.[48]

The US also agreed to supply substantial quantities of additional armaments, and to take further steps to help guarantee Israel's oil supplies. Finally, the US undertook to ensure the implementation of the Israel-Egypt peace treaty, thereby leading to the creation in the Sinai of the multinational peacekeeping force (the MFO) with its large US contingent. The net effect of all of this would be a tremendous increase in the number of Americans working on projects in Israel or committed in some way to ensuring Israel's security.

One other important consequence of the growing US involvement in Israel during the 1970s was the institutionalization of a defense dialogue between the two countries. While this was a far cry from the relationship that would develop during the Reagan Administration, the dialogue contributed to better understanding between the two countries and created a precedent for future discussions covering sensitive areas.

This dynamic first began in 1974, following the increase in US aid in the wake of the Yom Kippur War. Given the increasingly large amounts of aid involved, there was a natural interest in trying to rationalize the planning process and to better understand the concerns of both sides. So, in August 1974 Israel provided a list to the US of its defense needs for the next five years, and a general outline of needs for a further five. While the list would be greatly revised in the course of discussions over the next year, it marked the beginning of long-term planning on defense issues between the two countries.

This period also marked the beginning of a more visible role for the Israeli defense minister in US-Israel relations. In September 1974 Defense Minister Shimon Peres visited Washington to carry out a detailed review with Secretary of State Kissinger. He would become a frequent guest in Washington, insofar as both sides agreed that there was a real need for close and continuing dialogue covering defense-related issues.[49] Prior to this, the only such dialogue had been limited to intelligence contacts and discussions with military attaches.

Periodic discussions were subsequently held involving the Pentagon's Office of Net Assessment and the IDF Planning Branch. At first the dialogue primarily involved explaining Israel's strategy and the background to its requests for military aid. Gradually the broader security picture, including the role of the Soviets, also was addressed, although never in operational terms. While the dialogue has been described as primarily "academic" by Israeli officials, it represented the first time that the two sides talked about problems beyond the immediate day.[50]

The dialogue survived the changeover in governments in both countries in 1976 and 1977 and evolved, at least for the Israeli side, into a forum for addressing possibilities for cooperation that might serve both sides' interests. Increasingly the topic of discussion was the Soviets who, by the latter half of the 1970s, appeared to pose a real threat to the Middle East region. According to then Deputy Defense Minister Mordechai Zippori, who was in charge of the talks for the Israeli side beginning in 1977, the Israelis were interested in exploring a number of ways that the two countries could work together to thwart Soviet designs, including prepositioning, medical cooperation, and weapons maintenance.[51] While these ideas would be well received just a few short years later, the Carter Administration was not interested.

On the Eve of Revolution

Thus, whatever else might be said about the peace process of the 1970s, without doubt it made a powerful, if inadvertent contribution to the adoption of strategic cooperation during the 1980s. The huge amounts of US aid going to Israel, the many collaborative projects between the two sides that would bring not only money but people to Israel, and the growing perception that cooperation with Israel did not have to be at the expense of the Arab states — all of this created a certain logic and momentum in the US-Israeli relationship.

Meanwhile the political climate in the United States had created a solid bottom-line to US-Israel relations, below which the relationship was not likely to fall in the absence of a wholesale change in American popular opinion about Israel. Time and again in the 1970s the power of domestic politics made itself felt in the form of support for arms sales to Israel. In 1975 the Ford Administration tried to cut aid to Israel as a means of bringing pressure to bear on Jerusalem; the effort failed, in large part because it flew in the face of political realities in Washington.

The foreign policy bureaucracy, all in all, remained critical of Israel. But even here important changes were taking place, and it was no longer accurate to describe any particular institution as inherently hostile to Israeli interests. In part this reflected the societal changes that had begun in the United States in the 1960s and would eventually sweep through even the most traditionbound institutions, such as the Department of State. Additionally, as the United States became more involved in the Middle East, the pool of people covering the region necessarily grew and began reflecting a greater variety of perspectives and expertise.

Yet it was still not clear how Israel fit into broader US strategy in the region. Yes, there was bedrock domestic support for Israel which, at heart, was emotional, moral and principled. But when it came to crafting US strategy for the region, Israel's specific role depended on relevant US policy objectives at the time, whether these involved countering the Soviets or improving US relations with the Arab world.

Israel's strategic value was perceived to be high in the early 1970s when the Soviets were directly involved in the region. Later in the decade, as the strategic objective shifted toward achieving a US-brokered regional peace, Israel was perceived to be of reduced strategic value to the United States. The reality, of course, was that Israel was at the forefront of US calculations in both cases because of its ability to deny or ensure US objectives. Moreover, although "strategic" is most often defined in terms of helping to counter the Soviets, if one were to judge Israel's worth to the United States on the basis of tangible rewards (i.e., aid and commitments), US policymakers clearly saw Israel's strategic role in the realm of peace as equivalent in importance to its strategic role vis-a-vis the Soviets.

This paradox would leave an important legacy for the 1980s. On the one hand, in the world of perceptions people would search for a specific role that Israel could play vis-a-vis American strategic, meaning military, interests in the area. On the other hand, policymakers charged with crafting an American strategy for the entire region would view the issue of Israel's "strategic worth" in terms of its contribution to a variety of objectives, including peace.

Thus, on the eve of the new decade, an overall lack of clarity characterized the approach to Israel, its strategic value, and the nature of the strategic relationship that might exist between it and the United States. Certainly it was appreciated that a strong Israel was in the US interest. But whether this was intended to ensure that the US would never be faced with the contingency of massive intervention on Israel's behalf, or for coaxing Israel's cooperation on the peace process, or to play an active role in the region itself, was not clear. The 1970s left legacies in support of all three.

Yet the end of the decade also saw Washington reluctant to touch the idea of an alliance between the two countries. The logic of the increasing web of ties between the two countries pointed to a closer relationship. But it was canceled out by traditional concerns about US interests in the Arab world, combined with the Carter Administration's intense unhappiness with the Begin government.

Thus a key issue of the 1980s would be to define the type of alliance — defense treaty, strategic cooperation, or something else — that was required. Along the way, certain spin-off realities occurred that took on an importance of their own as aid, commitments, and the defense dialogue were all enhanced. All these factors would become crucial determinants for the decision in the 1980s as to whether to further expand military cooperation between the two sides.

Chapter 2. The Reagan Revolution

The Soviet Threat Reemerges

The 1980 presidential campaign served to redefine the nature of the US-Israeli relationship in terms that continue to reverberate a decade later. Candidate Ronald Reagan took the jump that no public official had yet been willing to take, and openly declared Israel to be an important ally of the United States and a major strategic asset.[1] Independent candidate John Anderson was not far behind in declaring Israel's importance and, by the end of the campaign, beleaguered President Carter had also reluctantly emphasized the strategic importance of Israel.

This was in sharp contrast to the previous administration's emphasis on the moral underpinnings of the US-Israeli relationship. Now, even though both major party platforms referred to America's moral obligation to Israel, the Democratic Party went on to describe Israel as a strategic asset and America's closest ally in the region. The Republican platform went even further to highlight the "deterrent role" of Israel's armed forces both in the Middle East and, most importantly, in East-West military equations.[2]

Domestic politics clearly were at work here, with the candidates competing for important voting blocs in key states. Even more important, however, was the charged international situation that had developed as a result of the Iranian revolution, an increase in terrorism, and the Soviet invasion of Afghanistan. In light of these events and widespread concern that the Soviet military machine would march on to new conquests, the 1980 campaign naturally tended to focus not on peace but on security. And, in a world divided into white and black, allies and enemies, Israel came up wearing a white hat.

The campaign thus represented an important hallmark in the long-festering debate over Israel's strategic significance to the United States. Yet aside from assertions about Israel's strategic importance, the debate as to how exactly Israel might help the US had not advanced significantly from the 1970s. The heart of the problem was, as it had been in the past, what role Israel could play in the region, given US interests in the Arab world. The Republican

Party platform — perhaps inadvertently — alluded to this dilemma when it pledged, right after its ringing support for Israel, to pursue "close ties" with moderate Arab states.[3]

But the debate in the past had also been somewhat academic inasmuch as, until the late 1970s, there was no real perceived weakness in the US military posture that could be filled by Israel. The fall of the Shah's regime in Iran and the Soviet invasion of Afghanistan changed all that. Suddenly there was an enormous gap — both perceived and real — in the US ability to ensure security in the region.[4] Whether and how Israel might assist in closing that gap became an issue not just for traditional regional planners but also for the new breed of American Cold War strategists, seized with crafting a global US response to what they saw as a global Soviet challenge.

The Reagan Administration inherited the Rapid Deployment Force (RDF) that was established in 1979 to provide the capability to respond quickly to events in the region. However, President Reagan also inherited the seemingly built-in weaknesses of that concept: lack of secure military access ashore and an unwillingness on the part of key Arab states to be seen as cooperating too closely with the American plan. By the beginning of Reagan's term, the most the US had been able to achieve with regard to access were understandings and agreements for contingent rights of access with Egypt, Kenya, Somalia and Oman.[5] Meanwhile, the perceived threat to the region had actually grown and, by 1981, revolved around the scenario of a Soviet land invasion of Iran.

Against this backdrop of an acute Soviet threat and weaknesses in the US ability to confront it, the case for relying on Israel was compelling: not only was Israel's military infrastructure sophisticated and its forces fully developed, but it also saw itself as an integral part of the western world; hence, it was reliable. While Israel's location was not as attractive as Saudi Arabia's, it was far better than sites the US actually had access to. Perhaps most attractive, Israel was quite willing to grant the US access to its military facilities.

Proponents of this point of view also offered a strong case for how a US-Israeli alliance would increase US political capital in the area. One of the more extreme voices making this argument was

Joseph Churba, head of the conservative Center for International Security in Washington. Deriding the Carter Administration for pandering to what he termed Arab bluffs, Churba urged Washington to "emphasize bilateral relations and bilateral security arrangements, even in open defiance of Arab or Moslem bloc priorities."[6] Far from undercutting US interests, Churba argued that only US strength would eventually convince the Arab states to be cooperative. Short of this, Churba warned of paralysis that would allow pro-western states "to be picked off one by one by Soviet adventurism or by Soviet-backed subversion."

The case against greater reliance on Israel argued exactly the opposite: that closer coordination would come at the expense of US options with the Arabs. Without a doubt, the importance of Saudi Arabia and other moderate Arab states outweighed the importance of Israel with regard to planning the defense of the Gulf. This was not only due to geographical and resource considerations, but also because of the presumed political costs that would accompany any Israeli involvement and thus undercut whatever limited military benefits might have been derived.

US failure to elicit the necessary cooperation of Saudi Arabia had to be at least partly blamed, according to this more traditionalist point of view, on the already close identification of US and Israeli interests and the refusal of the Israeli government to find a solution to the Palestinian issue. Thus, as one respected former US statesmen framed the issue on the eve of Reagan's entry into office, the options for US policy were either to force Israel to achieve peace or to distance itself from Israel, including by reducing aid.[7] Otherwise, Washington risked total isolation in the region.

Ronald Reagan clearly found the case for a US-Israeli alliance more attractive. It was consistent with domestic political realities in the United States which, as noted in the last chapter, had created a bedrock core of support for Israel. Reagan himself appears to have been personally sympathetic with the Israeli nation, remembering the early images of the death camps in Europe and admiring the victories that later shaped the new state. But most important, it was consistent with his Cold Warrior instincts, which seconded everything to the objective of fighting communism using whatever assets might be available.

Heady Days

Reagan's election thus ushered in a period full of promise for US-Israel relations. The key position of secretary of state went to Alexander Haig, considered a long-time friend of Israel dating back to the Nixon Administration. And while other appointments, such as that of Secretary of Defense Weinberger, were not quite so much to Israel's liking, all of the key appointments affirmed the basic anti-Soviet thrust of the administration.

Translated into policy toward the Middle East, this meant a downplaying of the Palestinian issue and an open mind as to Israel's role in the region. As Alexander Haig would later comment, "the tendency to focus on the Palestinian issue distracted the West from consideration of the fact that many Middle East conflicts, and especially those around the Gulf, had little to do with Israel and could not be solved by Israeli concessions."[8] Further, as the administration became preoccupied with state-sponsored terrorism, there was a natural inclination to look at forms of cooperation with Israel.[9]

This was welcome news for the government of Menachem Begin, which had tried and failed to convince the Carter Administration of Israel's strategic importance. Prime Minister Begin had long been warning of the dangers of an unchecked Soviet threat in the region and Israel's value in combatting it. Now he lost no time in expressing his hopes as to where US policy was heading. In an interview with a major American television network in November 1980, he made it clear that he believed the US should rely on Israel in crafting a new security policy vis-a-vis the region. In an earlier interview, he stated that the US was welcome to use Israeli military facilities and urged that US forces be deployed in the area to ensure a fast and effective US response to events in the Persian Gulf.[10]

Begin also expressed his hope for the formalization of closer defense relations with Washington, possibly in the form of a defense treaty.[11] Although he often stated that Israel would not request such a treaty from the United States, Begin left no doubt that, should the US broach the subject with Israel, he favored a formal alliance that included a defense pact. While President

Carter had not been interested in the idea (in large part because Begin had argued that he was not requesting American security guarantees in exchange for Israeli withdrawal from the Territories), the new administration's preoccupation with the Soviet Union seemed to open the door to many new possibilities.

Initial signs from the administration did indeed seem positive. In introducing its plan for foreign assistance to the Middle East in March 1981, Haig highlighted Israel's importance to Washington's developing regional strategy, stating that "Israel constitutes an important deterrent in the region, and indeed can play a major role in countering the more serious threats involving the Soviet Union itself."[12] This went far beyond previous annual statements justifying aid to Israel, and set an important tone for the way in which the Reagan Administration would approach Israel.

Moreover, the military dialogue begun in the 1970s between the US and Israel seemed finally to be paying off. Early in the administration, Israeli Deputy Defense Minister Mordechai Zippori returned from meetings in Washington excited by the understanding of Israel's position exhibited by the new administration. "All the people I met with — Defense Secretary Weinberger and his aides, the secretary of the navy, the secretary of the air force, the secretary of the army and others, with no exception — have an entirely different attitude toward Israel and the region and Israel's role in the US global concept."[13]

Meanwhile, efforts began to spell out exactly what it was that Israel could do for the US. For example, the RAND Corporation, in analyzing possible host nation support in the Middle East for the RDF, concluded that Israel had a crucial role to play for the US in any race to the Gulf.[14]

But there was still the troublesome issue of whether and how closer US-Israeli cooperation could be reconciled with competing US objectives vis-a-vis the Arab world, particularly Saudi Arabia. Testifying to the supreme importance that the administration attached to Saudi Arabia's cooperation, one of the first acts of the Reagan Administration was to recommend to Congress the sale of an arms package to Saudi Arabia, including five AWACS. Meanwhile, new arrangements for access in the region were evolving with both Saudi Arabia and Egypt, and military construction aimed at improving regional facilities in Egypt, Oman, Somalia, Kenya and Diego Garcia was accelerated to the tune of $2 billion.[15]

It fell to Secretary Haig to try to reconcile these urgent US military priorities with the US commitment for a closer, albeit undefined, US-Israeli alliance. Convinced that this could be done, Haig adopted an approach that came to be known as "strategic consensus." Simply put, it was an effort to get both Israel and the moderate Arab states to play on the same team by convincing both sides to subordinate regional sources of instability to the task of countering the common threat: the Soviets. (While Haig was to be proven wrong with regard to collaborative efforts the Arabs and Israel would be willing to swallow, he was instinctively right in thinking that both sides could show at least tacit understanding of the need for US cooperation with each.)

In April, Haig set off to the region to confirm support for this approach in Egypt, Saudi Arabia, Jordan and Israel. From the Arabs, he was essentially asking for patience regarding the Israeli-Palestinian issue. From Israel, he wanted understanding regarding the need to provide Saudi Arabia with sophisticated armaments, particularly the proposed AWACS sale. The responses were not encouraging. In both Saudi Arabia and Jordan, Haig was told that the United States should reassess its priorities, and that it was the Palestinian issue that provided the Soviets with their best opening in the region.[16] President Sadat, already isolated in the Arab world as a result of his peace agreement with Israel, also stressed the necessity for a broader peace process.

From Israel, Haig also got the message that trying to create a single unified team would not be easy. The Israeli leadership was beginning to be concerned that US preoccupation with the Soviet threat to the Gulf — only a few months earlier considered to be the path to a US-Israeli partnership in the region — might instead be leading to deeper US reliance on the Arab states. Giving voice to this concern, Foreign Minister Shamir argued that only Israel could be relied upon to resist the Soviets — the Arabs never would.[17]

Notwithstanding such differences over regional priorities, including the AWACS sale, the overall message that Haig delivered in Israel did nothing to discourage the Israeli leaders from thinking that the parameters for US-Israeli cooperation were wide open. Even if the US still did not specify what US-Israeli cooperation would consist of or how it would fit into the new anti-Soviet scheme, Haig left no doubt about the American commitment to deepening the US-Israeli alliance. In a presentation to the Knesset following the visit, Prime Minister Begin reported that Haig's visit had confirmed many points of agreement between Israel and the US: regarding the Syrian role in Lebanon, combatting terrorism, and opposition to Soviet expansionism and, most of all, that a "permanent alliance" existed between the two countries.[18] Begin would continue to refer to this alliance and his interest in formalizing it even as relations took a downward turn that summer.

The sum total of Haig's visit thus can be seen as further emphasizing the contradictions in US policy. The concept of strategic consensus had not been embraced and was quietly dropped. This left two trains increasingly pursuing independent courses. On the one hand was US reaffirmation of the importance of cooperating with moderate Arab states, complemented by Arab insistence that the US do something about Israel's stance in the region, particularly with regard to the peace process. On the other hand, the US had also reaffirmed the idea of a closer US-Israeli partnership that was premised not on peace but on security concerns vis-a-vis the Soviet Union.

Efforts to dance between these two competing interests became more difficult in the wake of Israeli military actions that summer. In June 1981 Israel attacked Iraq's Osiraq nuclear reactor, leading to a strong US rebuke and a decision to suspend F-16 deliveries to Israel. Following the attack, the State Department refused to describe the US and Israel as allies, preferring instead to talk of an alliance between the "peoples" of the two countries.[19] Just one month later, in a series of attacks on terrorist bases in Lebanon, Israel launched an airstrike on PLO headquarters in downtown Beirut. A number of civilians were killed in the attack, leading to US condemnation and, again, a suspension of F-16 deliveries (because US-supplied combat aircraft had been used in the raid).

On the surface, these actions did not sway the administration from its basic view of Israel's value to the United States. Indeed, some administration officials no doubt saw the bombings of both Iraq's nuclear facility and PLO headquarters as furthering US interests. But elsewhere questions were again raised as to what an Israeli-American alliance would consist of and how it would serve US interests.[20] It became clear that key elements of the administration sympathized with this concern when the test came, just a few months later, of finally working out the details of a new cooperative US-Israeli relationship.

Strategic Cooperation is Conceived

On September 9, 1981 Prime Minister Begin arrived in Washington, accompanied by Foreign Minister Yitzhak Shamir and newly-appointed Defense Minister Ariel Sharon, for his first formal meetings with President Reagan. Whatever differences had existed in the stormy period before, they were seemingly swept away during a visit that reporters would describe as the "warmest reception" ever given to Begin. Indeed, according to Begin, Secretary Haig's first words to him were about the need to put "everything that has happened until now behind us."[21]

According to accounts from both Israeli and US officials involved in the visit, the suggestion for some type of formalization of the US-Israeli relationship came from Prime Minister Begin. In the course of President Reagan's remarks during his first session with Begin, he repeated his oft-used line about the Soviet challenge and Israel's value as an ally. Begin, sensing that the talks were going smoothly, picked up on the reference to Israel as an ally and suggested that the concept be formalized. Reagan quickly, almost casually, seconded the motion, the two leaders joined the rest of their counterparts, and the project was turned over to the defense ministers.

The decision apparently took everyone by surprise. Defense Minister Weinberger was particularly unhappy with it and, as one senior American participant put it, "would put the Israelis through hell" during the subsequent negotiations.[22] Begin and Reagan's brief endorsement of the concept of formalizing their relationship did not extend to a meeting of minds over any of the specific details, such as whether this would be a written or unwritten agreement, or what it would cover. According to Begin's account of the meeting, the idea of a defense treaty was not raised by President Reagan.[23] But anything short of that seemed to be fair game.

Press briefings by both sides immediately following the announcement already hinted at different US and Israeli approaches. Initial briefings from Pentagon officials stressed that "low-level" opportunities for cooperation would be discussed, and that they did not see the need for a written memorandum of understanding.

In his own meetings with reporters, Begin sounded a very different note, saying that what he hoped for was a formal document that might include the following: the prepositioning of large amounts of US weaponry, including tanks, in Israel for emergency use by the RDF; the provision of an air cover umbrella by the Israel Air Force far into the Eastern Mediterranean to protect US transport airlifts as needed; American use of two new airbases in the Negev, including a new runway strictly for US use (capable of handling B-52 bombers); and use of port facilities at Haifa and Ashdod for docking, repairs and recreation.[24] Dismissing criticism by his Labor opponents that strategic cooperation "boiled down to the building of a few hospitals," Begin emphasized to Israeli audiences that "real" cooperation was under discussion, "the details of which are many and very serious and include cooperation on land, on the sea, and in the air."[25]

It would be left to the negotiators on both sides to try to reconcile these different approaches as to what cooperation should consist of. Working in their favor was an apparent agreement on the starting point: that the two sides would "present recommendations for spheres of cooperation to help deter Soviet aggression against the whole Mideast region." The US team would be headed by Under Secretary of Defense Fred Ikle, well-known for his tough views about the Soviet Union. The Israeli team would be headed by an Israeli general, Avraham Tamir, who held equally strong views about the nature of the Soviet threat.[26]

But despite an apparent commonality of views regarding the Soviets and notwithstanding the positive stance adopted by the Reagan Administration toward US-Israeli cooperation since the beginning of the year, it quickly became apparent that the US side wanted to limit any possibilities for real cooperation. What had happened to change attitudes so significantly? First, Weinberger was put in charge of the effort; he had made no secret of his opposition to a formal agreement with Israel. Secondly, in the wake of disagreements with Israel over regional policies, there was an increasing perception in Washington that, despite the bedrock political commitment to Israel, there were not many areas where the US wished to be seen as collaborating with it. Third, the differences that emerged in the course of the negotiations also exposed an unbridgeable gap between what Begin and Sharon wanted for Israel and what the US was willing to give them. Without a doubt, Israeli expectations for where strategic cooperation would lead were grandiose: Sharon envisaged Israel becoming a Middle East bridgehead for the defense of the free world. Begin saw it as the beginning of a truly genuine alliance with the US, based on mutual interests and equal status of both countries, possibly growing into a defense treaty. In contrast, the US had not given up its hope of creating a regional net of cooperative alliances. Far from steering the ship, as Israel appeared to desire, the US plan counted on Israel to simply not rock the boat.

Begin and Sharon

The Israeli approach to the MOU negotiations was shaped by two key individuals: Prime Minister Begin who, after his victory at the polls that summer, was more self-confident and driven than ever before, and Defense Minister Sharon, who believed that uncompromising strength and use of force were the key elements for Israel's security. Contrary to traditional Israeli caution in dealing with its major ally, the second Begin government seemed to have the "smug feeling that, for all intents and purposes, Washington was 'in Israel's pocket.'"[27]

Both Prime Minister Begin and Defense Minister Sharon shared the Reagan Administration's concern about the Soviet threat. For Begin, this probably stemmed as much from his experiences with Stalinist Russia on the eve of World War II, where he was imprisoned, as it did from Soviet actions in the region. Warnings about the dangers of Soviet expansionism were a constant theme in Begin's speeches, and there was clearly a meeting of minds between him and President Reagan about the threat that the Soviets posed to the free world.

But Begin also recognized the tactical utility of using the veneer of a Soviet threat to shroud any US-Israeli cooperation. In an interview with Israel Radio following his meetings with President Reagan, Begin explained that he had taken the lead in distinguishing between the defense of Israel against Arab threats and the common interests of both sides in standing up to Soviet expansionism. The first was a matter for Israel alone, the second for collaboration between two free and democratic nations. He stated that the American side was receptive to this line of argument, and he expected that it would "take this tack of explanation" in response to Arab complaints about cooperation with Israel.[28]

His sensitivity to the American need for a "cover" underscores that, for him, the fact of a formal cooperation agreement with the US was more important than the way it was characterized. Indeed, Begin was looking for an agreement with the US that would confer upon Israel a status that had long been lacking in the relationship. He had a deep sense of pride and clearly was uncomfortable with the notion that America was "helping" Israel for moral reasons alone. From his perspective, there had to be a sounder basis for relations, one that was grounded on a mutual perception of national self-interest.

This had become particularly important following the increase in US aid in the aftermath of the Camp David Accords, and in view of the fact that Israeli military leaders were already telling Begin that they would need even more US military aid in the 1980s and 1990s to keep up with developments in the Arab countries.[29] A strategic rationale that justified continued American largess on the basis of US self-interest thus seemed imperative. Appearing to take hand-outs was not only inconsistent with Israel's image of itself, it was also, from Begin's perspective, a totally false image, given all of the assistance that Israel had rendered to the US through the years.

Thus Prime Minister Begin repeatedly referred to the egalitarian nature of the US-Israeli relationship, as it was directed against a common Soviet threat, in the run-up to his meetings in Washington.[30] Israel was not solely on the receiving end of this relationship, but was a strong ally that contributed to the national security of the United States, including by blocking Soviet expansionism. His studied references to a defense treaty echoed this same theme. Such a treaty would serve to codify the roles that each side played in promoting the defense interests of the other — it would not be a quid pro quo for an Israeli withdrawal from the Territories.

Begin had good reason to believe that the US would approach the codification of strategic cooperation in a like manner. President Reagan had often expressed his belief that the US-Israeli relationship was a two-way street and, in early February, had stated that Israel's combat-ready and experienced military was "a force in the Middle East that actually is of benefit to us."[31] Secretary Haig was also clearly sympathetic to Israel's desire for equality. Testifying before a Senate committee in late September, he referred to the pride of the people in the region and remarked that it was no longer possible for the US to simply extend its presence around the world, but that it had to work with the local governments as "partners."[32] It was also Haig who, in recognition of Israeli sensitivities, stopped calling Israel a strategic "asset" and instead called it a "permanent ally and friend."

It is thus all the more ironic that, in the final analysis, the MOU of December 1981 failed to give Begin any of the status that he so desired. On the contrary, it became another example of the willingness of American political leaders to intervene to "help" Israel (as General Menachem Meron termed it) through a largely symbolic gesture rather than a genuine expression of ways in which both sides could equally help each other.

Defense Minister Sharon's interest in strategic cooperation was to achieve a broad-based document that would give practical meaning to a new role for Israel in the region. Unlike Begin's concern to achieve equality with the US, Sharon appears to have approached the negotiations from a genuine belief in Israel's superior abilities. And, in contrast to many Israelis, Sharon was quite willing to identify the Soviet Union as Israel's enemy, due to its activities not only in the Middle East, but around the globe.

While this like-minded preoccupation with the USSR should have facilitated the US-Israeli dialogue on strategic cooperation, in fact it helped to pull the two sides apart. Sharon was confident that President Reagan wanted "to incorporate Israel, and the IDF, into the effort to deter Russia and Russian surrogates from threatening the Near East and Africa."[33] Consistent with this, he brought maps and charts with him to Washington detailing the arc of Soviet influence spreading in Africa as well as the Middle East and Persian Gulf. The practical effect of his sweeping presentations was to argue for US-Israeli coordination throughout the region, including in Africa, against a pervasive Soviet threat.[34] While many of his American interlocutors no doubt shared his concerns, they undoubtedly were taken aback by the idea of such extensive US-Israeli collaboration. For, if accepted, it would have resulted in de facto collaboration against radical Arab states — Sharon's aim.

One particular area of concern for Sharon was the Persian Gulf and the Iran-Iraq War. The threat, from his perspective, was twofold: that Iraq would emerge a winner from the war and turn its attention to Israel, and that the Soviet Union would take advantage of a weak Iran to invade the country. Each scenario was dangerous for Israel; together, they provided a clear reason why Israel should be concerned with events in the Gulf. Sharon recounts how he repeatedly urged the US to maintain low-profile contacts with Iran and to avoid selling any arms to Iraq.[35] While some members of the administration would eventually find this line of argument appealing, in 1981 Pentagon planners tended clearly to see Iran as the chief enemy and Iraq as the lesser of two evils.

But it was a third aspect of dealing with the Soviet threat that no doubt alarmed Sharon's Defense Department interlocutors the most. In a September interview, Sharon reported that he had dwelt at length during his Washington discussions on his belief that US strategy in the region should be based on a preemptive deterrent rather than a deterrent of response.[36] In his view, the Afghanistan experience had shown the importance of seizing a troublespot before the Soviets moved in, thus shifting the dilemma of response to the Soviets. Israel could provide crucial facilities to the US in this regard. "It takes forty-eight hours to ship oranges and watermelons from Judea, Samaria (the West Bank) and Gaza to Saudi Arabia. In an emergency they (the US) could move tanks overland to support the Saudis in the same forty-eight hours."[37] Regardless of the theoretical merits of either the strategy or the plan, the emphasis on preemption no doubt set off alarm bells for US officials already concerned about Israeli actions in the region. Small wonder that, in the final document, the only area of possible cooperation that was explicitly spelled out was the Eastern Mediterranean. Even here, no concrete promises were made.

According to one of the Israeli participants in the negotiations, all parts of the Pentagon were opposed to the MOU: the Air Force, Army, Navy and, of course, Secretary Weinberger. One candid comment from a US military participant in the negotiations is instructive. When asked by an Israeli colleague why he was opposed to the MOU, his simple response was that, "we don't need it. The damage would be much greater than any benefit because of the Arab reaction."[38] Another US participant at the time stated that there was simply no strategic reason for the agreement. This was not hostility to Israel, according to the official, but the professional military's judgement that Israel did not have a genuine role to play in a global war with the Soviets, and could play only a negative role during a regional conflict.[39] The US military had other reservations as well about formalizing cooperation: fear that Israel would be given a "hunting license" to dip into US equipment stocks; a perception that the whole effort was being driven by political rather than strategic imperatives; and a feeling that formalization of cooperation was simply not necessary, given the proven track record of low-level cooperation that had worked effectively in the past. And, underlying everything else, there was concern not to appear to be collaborating in or approving of Israel's adventures in the region.

The negotiations underscored these concerns. A senior American diplomat recalled presenting the first draft of the MOU to Prime Minister Begin. As he started to describe the contents of the document — which dealt primarily with medical supplies and equipment — Begin cut him off and asked to read the paper himself. Looking up a few moments later, he asked the diplomat if he knew the story of "Unter den Linden." When the diplomat replied in the negative, Begin proceeded to explain that there once was a very beautiful Jewish girl who was also very poor. A German nobleman became quite taken with the girl and pledged her his undying love. The nobleman painted a beautiful picture of their future together, but when it came time for her to find out where they could meet the following day, he responded that they could meet anywhere but "under den linden" — in other words, not in Berlin's main thoroughfare, where they might be seen together. Begin remarked that that story seemed to describe the document he was holding.

Political Intervention in Washington

Only after Reagan and Haig intervened was the document made even minimally acceptable to the Israeli side. To some degree this intervention reflected the genuine differences that existed within the administration over Israel's role. It is important to recall that before the initiation of negotiations on the MOU, it was not only the Israelis but also elements within the administration that were talking about significant cooperation — including prepositioning of war reserve stocks, joint exercises, and contingency planning.

Indeed, on the eve of Begin's September visit, the US press reported (based on an interview by Haig and elaborations provided by unnamed officials) that Washington was considering an ambitious agenda for cooperation, including use of Israeli territory as a forward facility for the RDF.[40] The RAND report, referred to earlier, offered compelling reasons for greater reliance on Israel. There were clearly people positioned in the administration willing to listen. These included not only Secretary Haig, who had appointed several officials sympathetic to greater reliance on Israel (including Paul Wolfowitz and Harvey Sicherman), but also Director of Intelligence Casey, Jeane Kirkpatrick, and perhaps the national security adviser at the time, Richard Allen.

Even more important than the military considerations for those who supported strategic cooperation was the hope for significant collateral benefits in the form of altered Israeli policies. This was consistent with the school of thought which held that the best way to moderate Israeli policies was through closer relations — not turning away from Israel. Specifically, there was hope that strategic cooperation would yield important changes regarding Israeli restraint in the region, Israeli understanding of US initiatives such as the AWACS sale to Saudi Arabia, and Israeli willingness to pursue a peace process.

In the course of negotiations, however, it undoubtedly became clear that the Israeli team saw no need to "pay" for anything. As Sharon stated to a closed audience in Israel just before the September visit to Washington, "The time has come for us to stop standing like beggars at the door...Israel has much to offer to the US in terms of strategic cooperation and should state its case clearly."[41] The Israelis saw themselves as confident, independent players who were offering their advantages to the United States so as to strengthen both sides. A quid pro quo involving linkage to other issues was not part of the deal. Indeed, from the Israeli perspective, the point of strategic cooperation was exactly the opposite: because this was to be an equal partnership, the US would have even less ability to pressure Israel.

Begin had suggested as much during a July interview, when he was asked whether Jerusalem was ready to offer assurances regarding future actions now that Israel and the US were allies. "Completely negative," Begin responded. "If anybody should think, even should it occur to him to think that one sovereign country should consult another . . . about specific military operations in order to defend its citizens, that would be absurd."[42]

As for the AWACS issue, Haig himself describes how the administration believed Prime Minister Begin had agreed not to actively oppose the sale, and the administration's subsequent sense of betrayal when, during his talks on Capitol Hill, Begin spoke out against the sale anyway. Haig speaks of the seemingly "irreparable harm" that was done at the White House by Begin's actions, and later of the "downward spiral that had begun with the AWACS" dispute.[43] If Haig at one time saw a strategic cooperation agreement as a way to assuage Israeli concerns over deepening US relations with the Arabs, by the end of Begin's visit to Washington it appears that the AWACS deal had become primarily a negative issue coloring the US-Israeli relationship.

The MOU on Strategic Cooperation

The final document, although stronger than the "unter den linden" version, was not considered very serious on the part of most of the participants. If Weinberger's strategy had been to create a document where nothing was agreed except a built-in veto over future implementation, he had indeed been successful. The MOU carefully defined a threat that would trigger cooperation as one "caused by the Soviet Union or Soviet-controlled forces from outside the region introduced into the region" (see Appendix 1). This was a far cry from Sharon's urging for coordination throughout the region, since the language appeared to exclude even Soviet clients such as Syria and Iraq. Indeed, the MOU specifically stated that cooperation "is not directed at any state or group of states within the region."

The specific fields of cooperation were theoretically wide open: military cooperation, joint military exercises, joint readiness activities, and "other" fields, such as prepositioning.[44] But everything was subject to further agreement between the two sides; and that agreement would, in turn, have to pass the key litmus test of whether it was directed against countering a threat by Soviet forces "outside the region introduced into the region." The only theater of operations explicitly mentioned for possible cooperation in the way of joint exercises was the Eastern Mediterranean. According to one Israeli participant, this was put in to make the document minimally acceptable for Israel. It contrasted sharply with Israel's arguments that it had a role to play throughout the region, including in the Gulf.

The one tangible area of agreement for Israel involved cooperation in research and development and in defense trade, both of which were listed in the MOU as areas to be addressed by joint working groups. The joint statement following the signing ceremony on December 1 noted in its final clause that the secretary and the minister had "also addressed questions of US military assistance to Israel, including measures to make Israeli industry more competitive in bidding on US contracts." According to Haig, this was to involve some $300 million in potential benefits to Israel through Israeli arms sales for American armed forces.[45]

Final Impressions

As Cabinet members gathered around Prime Minister Begin's hospital bed, where he was recuperating from a broken leg, to vote on whether Sharon should travel to the US to sign the MOU, it was clear that the document left much to be desired. Prime Minister Begin was tired and in severe pain, and probably, given the final substance of the document, deeply disappointed. According to participants at the meeting, it fell to Sharon and a small group of supporters to defend the document. The one challenge to the document came from Foreign Minister Shamir, who expressed concern about Israel naming the USSR as an explicit enemy. But another minister firmly stated that such references were common practice and that the Soviet Union was listed as an enemy in 13 other American documents. In the face of such certainty, Shamir backed down, only to discover later (in the face of ridicule by the Opposition) that Israel was indeed the first country to have signed onto a document where the Soviet Union was explicitly named as the enemy.

Even though some of his own advisors described the document as "worthless," from Sharon's perspective, too much had been invested in the document — including his own ego and prestige — to walk away from it. He would subsequently state that the primary benefit of the agreement was "the fact that it tightened bilateral security ties and recognized in formal language the mutually important nature of the relationship."[46] It was at least a starting point and would almost certainly lead to increased US aid. In the end, this view held sway.

On December 1, 1981 the document was signed by Sharon and Weinberger, not in a public ceremony at the Pentagon as the Israelis had envisioned, but in a small private meeting from which reporters were barred. Thus, even in the end, Weinberger succeeded in orchestrating the event so that the least significance would be attached to it.

The reaction in Israel was swift, forcing Sharon to cut short his visit in Washington. A furious debate erupted in the Knesset, where opposition members charged that the accord dragged Israel into commitments far beyond its own defense needs and that it freed Washington from helping Israel against Arab countries. As Abba Eban described it, "against North Korea, we're (the US) beside you. But if you have a dispute with an Arab state armed head to toe, we're out of it."[47] Others protested that the explicit mention of the Soviet Union in the document would unnecessarily provoke Moscow, could jeopardize the fate of millions of Soviet Jews, and was an unprecedented departure from the norms of such international documents. Yitzhak Rabin declared that "America's part in the strategic cooperation agreement is not worth the paper it is written on."[48]

Sharon defended the document by pledging that Israeli troops would not be mobilized except in defense of Israel's existence and by stressing that implementation of the agreement would contain many benefits, many of which would be kept secret. Given the clear opposition to the MOU that existed within the US Defense Department, however, this seemed a doubtful proposition. Former Israeli ambassador to Washington Simcha Dinitz put his finger on the key problem when he noted that what was lacking in the strategic cooperation agreement was a common strategy — both regarding the region and with regard to Israel itself.[49]

Dinitz's words about the lack of a common strategy between the US and Israel would prove prophetic. On December 18, the US suspended the document in protest at Israel's decision to extend its civil jurisdiction to the occupied Golan Heights. That one act said more about how the administration viewed the MOU and its intended effect on Israeli actions than did all of the preceding negotiations.

The immediate and harsh reaction that followed from Jerusalem made it equally clear how little Israel ever understood what the US wanted from the document. In a sharp statement read to US Ambassador Lewis and then made public, Begin canceled the accord and stated that "the people of Israel have lived 3,700 years without a memorandum of understanding with America and will continue to live without it another 3,700 years." Giving vent to his frustration over the lack of equality between the two countries he asked, "Are we a vassal state of yours? Are we a banana republic? Are we fourteen-year-olds who, if we misbehave, we get our wrists slapped?"[50]

So in the end, as in the beginning, the significance of the new strategic alliance between the two countries (or the question whether one existed at all) was left in limbo. The only reason the MOU came to fruition at all was political intervention. The strategic imperative for the agreement had proved the most controversial aspect of the whole affair and seemed, in the end, to underscore the lack of a specific role for Israel in US defense planning, particularly in the Gulf.

On the other hand, for the first time in US-Israel relations, the principle of military cooperation between the two sides had been established and even formalized under the aegis of confronting the Soviets. Although not a defense treaty and despite being heavily caveated, the document was nevertheless a milestone. It would take another two years, however, before it could be fulfilled.

Chapter 3. The Lebanon Interlude

The Limits of the Soviet Threat

As the first year of the Reagan Administration drew to a close, it was clear that despite mutually reinforcing rhetoric and the commonality of a Soviet threat that should have brought the two sides together, the US and Israel did not in fact see eye-to-eye as to what a strategic relationship was all about. Begin hoped that Israel would become the linchpin of US strategy in the region. Washington saw strategic cooperation as a way to offset its moves toward the Arab states, to help encourage Israeli moderation in the region, and to counter the Soviets. However, this last objective seemed to have more of a rhetorical quality to it than a clearly delineated role for Israel.

Indeed, it appeared that the preoccupation with the Soviet threat, once seen as a great opportunity for Israel, was now being turned against Israeli interests. Instead of being the bulwark against Soviet expansionism, Israel was pressed to fit into an overall regional strategy involving moderate Arab states.

Interestingly, this found expression a year later, in late 1982, when Deputy Secretary of State Kenneth Dam went to Capitol Hill to argue against a Senate-inspired increase in aid to Israel. Far from portraying Israel as part of the effort against the Soviet Union, Dam warned that additional money for Israel would come at the expense of other US friends and allies, including Spain, Portugal, Turkey and Pakistan, thereby undermining US efforts to counter the Soviet threat in Southwest Asia.[1] While administration disgruntlement obviously reflected the state of US-Israel relations in the wake of the Lebanon invasion, the rationale used by Dam is revealing in that it shows how the "Soviet threat" could be manipulated either for or against Israel.

What, then, was strategic cooperation intended to achieve? If it was genuinely aimed against the Soviets, there was a need for reassessment in light of Israel's refusal to be a team player. If it was genuinely to rely on Israel's military capabilities in the region, those too had to be reassessed in view of the Pentagon's refusal to view Israel as an asset. And if it was to forge common approaches to regional issues, the biggest demonstration of failure on that score was just around the corner.

Despite these problems that occupied the expert foreign policy community in Washington, domestic support for Israel continued strong, US aid to Israel was very high, and the Reagan Administration, as defined by President Reagan himself, remained essentially sympathetic to Israel and convinced that a strong democratic Israel was very much in the interest of the United States.

Meanwhile, despite the 1981 fiasco over strategic cooperation, lobbying in Washington in favor of closer strategic ties remained intense. In 1982, AIPAC began publishing a series of pamphlets spelling out how Israel could contribute to US defense policies. The series eventually would cover Israel's potential help to the US Navy (by offering support facilities for the Sixth Fleet as well as assisting with realistic training opportunities), the US Air Force (through making facilities available and even assigning a role to Israel's Air Force), and to the US Army, by allowing it to preposition materiel in Israel, perhaps including a mechanized division, for deployment to the Gulf.[2]

Events in 1982, however, would completely overshadow any renewed arguments in favor of closer strategic ties between the US and Israel. As the Reagan Administration continued to be pulled in competing directions by its secretary of defense and its secretary of state, a new debate ensued over how best to influence Israeli actions — whether to "crack down" on Israel or to exert quiet pressure. As Weinberger had fumed following the de facto annexation of the Golan Heights by Israel: "How long do we have to go on bribing Israel? If there is no real cost to the Israelis, we'll never be able to stop any of their actions."[3]

Frustration with Israel was not limited to the Pentagon. Secretary Haig, after listening to Defense Minister Sharon rail at him during a visit to Jerusalem in early 1982, retorted that, "If you act like an ally, General, you'll be treated like one."[4] And, reflecting the personal animus toward Begin that, according to then-US Ambassador Samuel Lewis, was steadily growing in Washington, the prime minister was advised not to make a planned visit to Washington in January.[5]

In the absence of a single clear policy, administration officials tended to go their own way. In February 1982 Weinberger completed a 10-day swing through Saudi Arabia, Oman and Jordan, notably omitting Israel from the tour. His message: the US need for "more than one friend" in the region. Indeed, a senior administration official said on background during the trip that the US was getting tough with Israel and would no longer be "hostage" to Israeli interests.[6] As if to underscore this point, Weinberger indicated during his stopover in Amman that the US might sell F-16s and Hawk SA missiles to Jordan. Although President Reagan subsequently reassured Begin in a letter that Israel remained "America's friend and ally," he also referred to the US need to enhance its influence with other states in the region.[7]

But hope for closer cooperation was not dead. Haig and other administration officials continued to favor strategic cooperation, if only as a way to overcome or at least contain problems with Jerusalem. And serious problems indeed were looming just over the horizon. Israeli officials repeatedly warned during the first half of 1982 of pending military action in Lebanon if PLO activities there were not effectively halted.

Additionally, the continued viability of the peace agreement between Egypt and Israel lay in Israeli hands as the deadline for completing the Israeli withdrawal from Sinai fast approached. The autonomy talks had ground to a halt; following Sadat's assassination the previous fall, there was concern that the peace treaty itself could also break down. So it was that the completion of Israel's withdrawal from the Sinai on April 25, 1982 came as a tremendous relief, and helped to restore credibility to Israel and to lower US apprehensions about Israel's unpredictable behavior. Accompanied by pictures of Israeli settlers being forcibly removed, the withdrawal also created sympathy regarding the price that Israel had paid for peace with Egypt.

After the withdrawal, Israel's popularity in America reached a level that had previously been achieved only after the Yom Kippur War in 1973. Gallup found, in April and May 1982, that a majority of Americans (51 percent) sympathized with Israel, compared with only 12 percent who sympathized more with Arabs.[8] This message was not missed by the administration, which was also concerned that in the public perception President Reagan had become less committed to Israel since the start of his term in office.[9]

Thus it was perhaps no coincidence that, in early May, the administration was said to be ready to revive strategic cooperation with Israel. During a visit to Washington, Israeli Deputy Foreign Minister Yehuda Ben Meir held discussions with Under Secretary of State for Political Affairs Lawrence Eagleburger. While the primary US message was an effort to encourage Israeli restraint regarding Lebanon, this apparently was coupled with the "carrot" of strategic cooperation.[10] Eagleburger, whose realpolitik views would come to have an important effect on the US-Israeli relationship, was already in 1982 appreciative of the value of maintaining a quiet, close dialogue with Israel on a number of foreign policy issues.

But while forces in the US were moving in the direction of closer cooperation, events in the Middle East were pulling the two countries apart. When Defense Minister Sharon arrived in Washington later that month it was clear that he was no longer interested in near-term strategic cooperation with the US. With plans already laid for the Israeli action to destroy the PLO in Lebanon, Sharon saw such an agreement as primarily shackling Israel's freedom of action.

Thus, with the invasion of Lebanon just a few days away (following a Palestinian attack on the Israeli ambassador to Great Britain), all talk of reviving strategic cooperation was put on hold, seemingly indefinitely. Indeed, when Israel launched the invasion, all of the possible impulses for closer cooperation were turned upside down:

— domestic pressure for a closer alliance fell victim to the controversy of the war;
— The premise that US-Israeli cooperation was needed to achieve common strategic objectives in the region appeared ludicrous given the severe differences that arose over events in Lebanon; and
— Soviet involvement was, at least initially, minimal, thus reducing that time-honored rationale for cooperation.

Given these bleak prospects for strategic cooperation at the start of the war, it is ironic that in less than a year, closer cooperation with Israel would once again make a comeback, this time stronger than ever. Critics would later charge that this dramatic change was manipulated — driven not by genuine strategic concerns but by domestic politics. Others, heaving sighs of relief that the up and down days of the early Reagan Administration had come to a close, would argue that the US had finally come to realize that its interests lay in cooperating with Israel. To determine which interpretation is correct requires a closer look at the way Lebanon affected administration perceptions of Israel's strategic value.

Plummeting to the Depths

Military-to-military relations between the US and Israel, already strained as a result of personal animosities, deteriorated even further during the Lebanon conflict. For the first time since 1974, when working-level meetings were established between military representatives of the two countries, dialogue virtually ceased. The 1981 MOU, which would have provided a successor framework for dialogue, had been suspended. Relations between Defense Minister Sharon and the Pentagon had reached such a low point that when Sharon traveled to Washington in May 1982, his primary meetings were held with Secretary of State Haig. And, back in Israel, Sharon seemed determined to close off even working level contacts between the Israeli defense establishment and the American attaches: he repeatedly admonished "defense ministry officials and senior army officers to keep their distance from the diplomatic community."[11]

Meanwhile, events in Lebanon created significant friction between American soldiers and the Israel Defense Forces. In early July, with Israeli troops on the outskirts of Beirut, President Reagan decided to contribute a contingent of US Marines as part of a UN-sponsored multinational force (MNF) for peacekeeping in Beirut. In accordance with an American-brokered agreement in August, the MNF was charged with supervising (and protecting) the evacuation of PLO fighters as they departed Beirut. As the evacuation began in September, two ships of the US Sixth Fleet anchored outside Beirut harbor to escort the Palestinians out. Underscoring the tension and suspicion already existing between the US and Israeli military commands, the ships were given orders "to break out of the harbor by force, if necessary, and if the IDF opened fire, to fire right back."[12]

This particular MNF mission was completed successfully (and was executed without a US-IDF confrontation) — leading to its withdrawal from Lebanon in mid-September. But a new, more hostile phase involving American troops and the IDF would begin just days later. On September 14, the president-elect of Lebanon, Bashir Gemayel, was assassinated. That night, the Israeli army moved into West Beirut and stood by while Phalangist troops massacred hundreds of Palestinian civilians in the refugee camps of Sabra and Shatila. Shocked by the turn of events, the president quickly decided to return the MNF to Beirut and to support the establishment of an effective Lebanese government and withdrawal of foreign forces.[13]

Unfortunately for the MNF, it would be almost a year before any discernible progress was made toward withdrawal of any of the forces. Meanwhile, the close proximity in which American and Israeli soldiers were operating, their differing objectives, and the overall breakdown in relations between Weinberger and Sharon contributed to a downward spiral of relations between the defense establishments of both countries. Between January 5 and March 12, 1983, the US Commandant of the Marine Corps detailed eight instances in which the IDF harassed US forces.[14] Charges abounded that the Pentagon was refusing to allow any tactical coordination between US units and Israeli forces, including banning any communications links between US aircraft and the Israel Air Force operating in the same limited air space.[15] The hostility between the two forces came to be symbolized by a photo of an American Marine officer halting three Israeli tanks near US lines with his drawn pistol.

The Lebanese affair ended for the US more than a year later with a car bombing by terrorists that killed 241 marines. By that time Lebanon — and the Israeli role in it — had become a black spot for the American defense personnel involved. Although other elements in the administration had become interested in working with Israel to preserve what was left of US policy in Lebanon, the predominant view of the US military was that the US should avoid being associated in any way with Israeli actions in Lebanon, and that it needed no help from Israel. As one high-level defense official recalled, "We wanted Israel out. Period."

For his part, Defense Secretary Weinberger saw the events in Lebanon as bearing out the skepticism that had so shaped the 1981 Memorandum of Understanding on strategic cooperation. He did not share Israeli objectives in Lebanon, he was unhappy that US forces had to be deployed there, and he was deeply concerned that the situation would undermine what he saw as more important US objectives with the moderate Arab states.

Political Goodwill Also Evaporates

Even more important than the Defense Department view, which was critical of Israel even before Lebanon, the invasion eventually led to a significant deterioration of popular and political support for Israel.

The initial US reaction to the invasion was fairly low-key and even sympathetic to Israel. But this was due primarily to the efforts of one man, Secretary of State Haig, rather than reflecting a consensus within the administration. On June 9, with the administration ready to support a UN Security Council draft resolution condemning the Israeli operation, only Haig's personal intervention turned the decision around.[16] Haig recounts other examples of his struggles against "a foreign policy bureaucracy, overwhelmingly Arabist in its approach to the Middle East" and against administration officials determined to punish Israel.[17] Haig believed that the invasion had created a strategic opportunity to bring peace to Lebanon through the expulsion of the PLO and the Syrians, as well as of the Israelis. Tactically, he believed that only a continuation of Israeli military pressure would create the conditions for such a solution.

Haig's key interest was his desire to undercut Soviet policy in the region, particularly in the Syrian context. Israel's humiliating destruction of 87 Syrian combat aircraft with no Israeli losses early in the conflict had led to apparent discord in Soviet-Syrian relations, which Haig hoped the US could exploit. This concern was also shared by CIA Director William Casey, who angrily dismissed concern that the US was appearing as an accomplice to

Israel and instead demanded to know how the US could "turn the situation" to its national interest.[18] Thus, at least on the part of some administration officials, preoccupation with the big picture — driving the Soviets out — was more important than the regional problems that the Israeli invasion had created for US policy.

But this broader perspective on the crisis would be short-lived. For reasons not specifically related to the Middle East, Haig was forced to resign on June 25. Meanwhile, administration frustration was growing over the lack of responsiveness by Israeli leaders to US concerns and anger over Israel's war objectives which, with each passing day, turned out to be increasingly ambitious. According to Haig, the president's anger with Begin, fed by the even greater anger of Weinberger (who was reportedly exploring ways to cut off military deliveries to Israel) and others, seemed to grow day by day.[19] For his part, Begin remained as irascible as ever, at one point responding to a demand from President Reagan by stating that "Jews do not kneel but to God".[20]

Begin's personal credibility with Reagan was severely damaged as a result of discrepancies between what he said or promised and actual events on the ground. Time and again Sharon ordered military operations seemingly designed to undercut US mediation efforts. Perhaps the most egregious example occurred in mid-August 1982: On August 11, the Israeli Cabinet had approved in principle the US-brokered plan to evacuate the PLO. The next day, Sharon ordered the fiercest attack to date on Beirut, consisting of 12 hours of bombing and resulting in at least 300 dead.[21] Known as "Black Thursday," the attack's effect on President Reagan was electric. In an emotional call to Prime Minister Begin demanding an immediate ceasefire, Reagan went so far as to evoke the image of the Holocaust to protest the Israeli action — an image which sparked an even more heated reaction from Begin.

The successful removal of the PLO on September 1 should have served to heal some of the differences between the two sides. Instead, it ushered in an even worse clash of US and Israeli interests. Begin saw the expulsion of the PLO as a victory against terrorism, an opportunity to deal a blow to Palestinian aspirations in the Territories, and, perhaps least understood by the US, a tremendous victory for US interests. As Israeli Ambassador to

Washington Moshe Arens declared in an interview in early September, the Lebanon War had proven the superiority of western armaments over those of the USSR and had changed the entire balance of power between the US and USSR. Did the US appreciate these clear gains? Arens commented that only the future would prove "whether the US intends to repay us for these gains or to use them against us, to cooperate with us as strategic allies, or to pocket the profits and 'repay' us with a kick."[22]

The US answer was not long in coming. On the day of the PLO expulsion, President Reagan announced a peace plan that ran headlong into Begin's expectations regarding the fading of the Palestinian issue. The crucial point of the Reagan Plan was its call for "self-government by the Palestinians of the West Bank and Gaza in association with Jordan." Perhaps even more noteworthy than the substance of the proposal was the fact that the administration had not coordinated the plan with Israel in advance, but had discussed it with Jordan.

The peace plan came to symbolize the seemingly total lack of identification of views between the US and Israel, not just over events in the region but also over the shape of a future Israel. Moreover, compared with the previous intense differences within the administration over Middle East policy, this time the administration was united: the president, vice president, newly-appointed Secretary of State George Shultz, Secretary of Defense Weinberger and National Security Advisor Clark all supported the new approach.

The plan was quickly and harshly rejected by the Israeli Cabinet as a deviation from the principles of Camp David. Meanwhile, despite Israeli and US hopes that the Lebanon War was over, Gemayel's assassination just two weeks later triggered the Israeli decision to enter West Beirut in violation of a commitment to President Reagan, followed by the Sabra and Shatila massacres. US-Israel relations seemed to hit rock-bottom. The US had given its assurances at the time of the PLO expulsion that the remaining Palestinian camps would be safe. That American promise had been broken; regardless of any direct culpability for the killings, Israeli troops controlled the area.

Not surprisingly, the sense of betrayal and revulsion felt by the administration came to be reflected in US public perceptions. That fall, Israel's rating as either a "close ally" or "friend" of the United States dropped by as much as 12 percentage points below prewar levels.[23] And, since the US and Israel seemed committed to continuing their sharply divergent policies with regard to both Lebanon and the peace process, "more of the same" seemed likely for the future. The label of "ally" did indeed seem very far off the mark; the concept of strategic cooperation seemed even further away.

Part II

Chapter 4. Strategic Cooperation Becomes Reality

The Long Road Back

Four factors would gradually lead to a dramatic improvement in US-Israel relations following the Lebanon debacle. First, three key personalities would either be replaced or would undergo a significant change in views, and the National Security Council would play a more important role in US-Israel relations. Secondly, the failure of US policies in the region would lead to a reassessment of ways to achieve US interests in the Middle East. Third, the Soviet Union would reemerge as a much more potent factor in US strategy in the Middle East. Finally, domestic pressures would build for an improvement in US-Israel relations.

The first key personnel change had immediate and positive effects for the relationship: in February, Israeli Defense Minister Ariel Sharon was removed as a result of the findings of the Israeli commission investigating the Sabra and Shatila massacres and was replaced by Moshe Arens, then Israeli ambassador to Washington. Sharon's penchant for flouting US concerns had only seemed to increase following those dark days in September 1982. Incidents between the US peacekeeping force and the IDF increased, and Sharon created endless obstacles to US mediation efforts between Israel and Lebanon, e.g., by embarking on secret talks with the Gemayel government designed to shut the US out. Former Ambassador Sam Lewis has remarked that Sharon seemed to have a compulsion to humiliate the United States.[1] It had become practically impossible to separate US-Israel relations from the bad blood between Washington and Israel's leaders, particularly Sharon. In mid-October, Foreign Minister Shamir had traveled to Washington for his first meetings with Secretary Shultz and reported a "certain calming" in relations.[2] But any progress that the Shamir visit might have been able to make was subsequently undercut by Defense Minister Sharon's activities in Lebanon.

Sharon's replacement by Moshe Arens thus was crucial in allowing both capitals to get beyond personalities and refocus on whatever mutual interests existed between the two countries.

Arens was everything Sharon was not: low-key, hard-line but civil, sensitized to American concerns and to Washington's approach to policymaking, and convinced of the necessity of working with Washington rather than against it. This last difference was perhaps the most important. Compared with Sharon's grandiose views of Israel's role in the region that tended to treat US interests as secondary concerns, Arens' view of the world was much more pragmatic. Gone were the sweeping rhetoric and visions. In their place was an almost bureaucratic perspective on what it would take to keep Israel strong.

The second key personnel change would be Begin's eventual replacement as prime minister by Yitzhak Shamir. Although the change would not occur until August 1983, Begin's central role in Israeli foreign policy was already fading by early 1983 as he grew listless and depressed following his wife's death the previous November. Greater control over Israeli policy thus fell to Shamir who, like Arens, approached foreign affairs from a practical day-to-day perspective rather than a sense of history-in-the-making. Although not so well-tuned as Arens to the intricacies of American politics, Shamir's low-key and cautious manner would also help smooth the way for improvement in US-Israel relations.

The third key change in personality would be the transformation of Secretary of State George Shultz. Shultz's appointment in the wake of Haig's forced resignation was widely seen in Israel as unfavorable: Shultz, like Weinberger, had worked for the Bechtel Corporation, which had major concerns in the Arab world. During Shultz's confirmation hearings, the central conclusion that he drew from the Lebanon conflict was that "the legitimate needs and problems of the Palestinian people must be addressed and resolved, urgently and in all their dimensions."[3] One of his first activities as secretary of state was the fashioning of the new peace plan that so took Israel by surprise on September 1.

In view of Begin's harsh rejection of the Reagan Plan, coupled with deteriorating conditions in Lebanon, Shultz turned his attention to gaining Arab support for the plan, particularly from Jordan and Saudi Arabia. During a visit to Washington by the Jordanian monarch in late 1982, President Reagan offered several incentives — including the sale of F-16s — if the King would enter the peace process.⁴ State Department support for Weinberger's idea of creating a Jordanian rapid deployment force also seemed premised on King Hussein joining the peace process.⁵ By the end of 1982, this resulted in the unusual spectacle of a united administration effort to persuade Congress not to increase aid to Israel so as not to send the wrong signal to the Arabs.

Yet in less than a year, George Shultz would be the key architect of a close US-Israeli relationship that would last for the rest of the Reagan Administration. What happened to Shultz? Simply put, his hopes regarding the Arab states drastically plummeted, at the same time that his estimation of Israel rose significantly. Syria, rather than Israel, came to be seen as the key obstacle to achieving a withdrawal of foreign forces from Lebanon; King Hussein, rather than Prime Minister Begin, was now perceived as unwilling to commit to peace.

The clearest turning point was Shultz's dip into personal diplomacy in the spring of 1983. Already his views about the region had begun to change: in the wake of Sharon's ouster, the quality as well as the tone of US-Israel relations had improved dramatically, and Shultz was developing confidence in and respect for the Israeli leadership. This was due in part to the education Shultz was receiving from Robert Ames, the CIA's chief analyst on the Middle East. Ames was intimately familiar with the murky and violent world of Beirut, and could explain in understandable and sympathetic terms Israel's objectives and tactics there.

In mid-April, US goals in the region — withdrawal of foreign forces from Lebanon and a viable peace process involving Israel and Jordan — had reached a critical stage. Certainly the bombing of the American Embassy in Beirut on April 18 drove home the message that something had to be done to break the deadlock in Lebanon. Robert Ames happened to be at the Embassy when the explosion occurred and was killed along with 60 others, among them the CIA station chief and deputy station chief.⁶

As Shultz embarked on a mission that would take him to Egypt, Israel, Lebanon, Jordan, Syria and Saudi Arabia, both professional and personal reasons strengthened his determination to achieve progress regarding the twin problems of Lebanon and the Arab-Israel conflict. By the end of the trip he believed that he had achieved success with regard to both objectives. As a result of his shuttle diplomacy between Jerusalem and Beirut, a peace agreement between the two countries was finally completed and was approved by the Israeli Cabinet on May 6. With regard to the peace process, Shultz believed that he had gained the King's support for the Reagan Plan during his talks in Jordan.

The subsequent denouement in both cases frustrated and infuriated Shultz. Syria's refusal to leave Lebanon and the ultimate repudiation of the agreement by the Lebanese government meant the unraveling of the peace treaty. What he thought had been a commitment from King Hussein, made during a cruise aboard the royal yacht, to participate in the peace process, turned out upon Shultz's return to Washington to be far less. What had begun as hope that the Reagan Plan would be given new life, turned into a frustrating lesson in the Arab diplomatic ploy of avoiding open confrontation, thereby making it difficult for outsiders to pin their Arab interlocutors down on any given issue.

The contrast with Shultz's experiences in Israel could not have been drawn more sharply. Although the Shultz-brokered peace treaty came close to not being approved by the Israeli Cabinet, the debate and the issues were all up front — not much is left to the imagination in Israeli diplomacy. Shultz appreciated this. Somewhere in the course of the five visits he made to Israel during his shuttle diplomacy with Lebanon, Shultz developed a seemingly genuine enthusiasm for Israel. As he reported in a speech upon his return to Washington, "It was an extraordinary experience for me on the personal level. The government and people of Israel, who have yearned so long for acceptance and for security," had finally achieved it.[7] Later in the year, as it became clear that the agreement was a dead letter, Shultz expressed disbelief that the peace agreement had proved so contentious on the Arab side. "What's so unreasonable about the agreement? It seems damn reasonable to me."[8]

The nature of his comments regarding the peace process underwent a similar change. In an apparent allusion to Jordan, Shultz stated upon his return from the region that the Arabs bore a special responsibility not to miss the chance for peace. By the end of year, the shift in responsibility had become even more pointed, with Shultz stating that he believed that if an Arab leader were to come forward to negotiate, "Israel would be there."[9]

This shift in perspective, borne of frustration in the first instance, was buttressed by a growing sense of ease and identification of interests with Israel. Central to this, and unique to George Shultz, was the personal interest that he developed in Israel's economy. Ten years after the 1973 war, Israel's "economic Yom Kippur" struck.[10] The Israeli economy staggered under the burden of a growing national debt and an annual inflation rate approaching 400 percent. An economist himself, Shultz became intrigued intellectually with finding ways to redress Israel's serious problems, and came to enjoy his frank and stimulating discussions with his Israeli counterparts on this issue. It became yet another subject drawing the two sides together.

The transformation of George Shultz was key to a gradual but thorough change in administration strategy toward the region. After a long hiatus — perhaps from as far back as 1970 — mutual interests were identified between the US and Israel in the region, starting with Lebanon. The dialogue between the two countries expanded tremendously as high-level visitors traveled back and forth. On May 20, 1983, the sale of 75 F-16s to Israel was approved.

Still, in a manner reminiscent of the first year of the Reagan Administration, a clear consensus did not suddenly develop in favor of closer cooperation with Israel. Rather, what Shultz's transformation signaled was the reemergence of the policy dispute within the administration over Israel's role in US regional strategy.

Strategic Cooperation: Debate II

The change in players had an enormous effect on the way the second debate over strategic cooperation was waged. For starters, Shultz was a much more effective player than Haig had been. He enjoyed the president's trust and had a great deal of stature that carried over into Cabinet-level debates. On the Israeli side, the personnel changes that had already made possible the improvement of bilateral relations, also greatly affected prospects for a renewal of strategic cooperation.

Compared with 1981, there were no regional military adventures by Israel looming on the horizon to complicate relations. Indeed, in the face of mounting losses, Israel decided unilaterally to pull its forces back to southern Lebanon during the summer of 1983. Testifying to the degree of change that had taken place, the administration now sought to delay the withdrawal out of concern that chaos would follow and the Marines would be overexposed.

Even more important for the outcome of the second debate was the context in which it was conducted. Whereas Gulf security had been of paramount concern in 1981, in 1983 terrorism and the taking of hostages came to obsess the administration like no other issue. In the face of US government inability to get a grip on the problem and its impotency to punish the aggressors, more and more time would be spent on problems like thinking of ways to pursue Muammar Qadhafi, Libya's radical leader and a supporter of international terrorism. The current of countering terrorism would eventually run through practically all aspects of US foreign policy.

What this meant for Israel was an increasing preoccupation on the part of the Reagan Administration with a region (the Eastern Mediterranean littoral states) and an issue (countering terrorism), both of which involved Israel. Lacking in the 1981 debate had been a genuine sense of urgency as to how strategic cooperation with Israel would benefit the United States. After efforts to assign Israel a role in the Gulf had failed, proponents of strategic cooperation really did not have a fallback position as to what Israel could do for the US, except for a vague sense of countering Moscow. Now, in 1983, as the US began laying plans for dealing with the terrorist threat both in Lebanon and in Syria, Israel had an obvious role to play both through intelligence cooperation and by the example of its own struggle against terrorists.

Not that combatting terrorism became the heart of strategic cooperation as it evolved at the end of the year. But in that critical period, as the administration once again debated how close relations with Israel should be and how Israel should fit into broader regional objectives, the war against terrorism created an atmosphere highly conducive to closer cooperation with Israel.

This was particularly true at the NSC. Following William Clark's resignation in October 1983 and his replacement as NSC advisor by Bud McFarlane, the NSC increasingly supported the use of US military force in pursuit of American foreign policy objectives. This meant support for friends in the region who could contribute to US undertakings. This was by no means limited to Israel: US-Egyptian coordination was enjoined with regard to possible joint operations against Libya, and US-Saudi cooperation increased on a number of fronts, including Saudi willingness to funnel money to the Nicaraguan Contras. This new activism at the NSC would play a pivotal role in the final decision on strategic cooperation in November 1983.

Further contributing to the new environment regarding Israel's role was a perceived heightening of the Soviet menace. Moscow's downing of a KAL civilian airliner on September 1, 1983 marked a low point in US-Soviet relations. The arms control talks broke down that fall and the "arc of crisis" brought on by Soviet activities around the globe dominated US decisionmaking. One important aspect of this was the appearance of the Soviet threat at Israel's back door. In late 1982, following the poor performance of the Syrian air defense system during the Lebanon War, the Soviet Union began a massive arms buildup in Syria. In short order it deployed the SA-5 surface-to-air missile, along with other sophisticated equipment and some 7,000 Soviet technicians.

As in the past, the Soviet threat cut both ways for Israel. The traditional point of view, represented by Weinberger, held that the US had to improve its relations with the Arab states in order to contain Soviet influence, and that US policy toward Israel should reflect this more important priority. This theme was reflected by the State Department's Assistant Secretary for Near East Asian Affairs Nicholas Veliotes during testimony on Capitol Hill regarding the administration's foreign aid requests. The justification for aid to Israel focused primarily on the need to reassure Israel and to maintain its technological edge; the passing reference to Israel's strategic value was vague, as had become standard with US officials. The justification for aid to Egypt, on the other hand, highlighted the mutual Egyptian and American concern over threats from the Soviet Union and the joint military cooperation which stemmed from this shared concern.[11]

But for proponents of closer cooperation with Israel, including Secretary of State Shultz, the Soviet buildup in Syria meant that the specter of the Soviet threat had moved from the Gulf to the heartland of the Middle East. This was somewhat reminiscent of the early 1970s when Henry Kissinger, faced with a Soviet presence in Egypt, sought to emphasize relations with his own client state — Israel — so as to counter the Soviets and encourage Egypt to move into the western camp. Now, more than 10 years later, with a growing Soviet presence in the region and Soviet support for the destabilizing activities of its client, the solution again seemed to be to build up the US side of the equation in order to counter Moscow and induce a more cooperative Syrian posture in the region. Kissinger's hope in the early 1970s was to create new options vis-a-vis Egypt; he was successful. The strategy in 1983 was to try to create similar options vis-a-vis Syria.

Under Secretary of State Lawrence Eagleburger, who had worked with Kissinger, was one of the most forceful proponents of this realpolitik strategy against Moscow. In an address in June, Eagleburger noted that "Israel stands as a bastion of Western interests and values in an area perpetually coveted by the Soviet Union.... Its military power is seen by the Soviets as standing in the way of their expansionist ambitions in the Middle East. The security of Israel is a vital American interest, and we will not stand idly by in the face of Soviet threats to that security."[12] His conclusion was a throwback to the early rhetoric of the Reagan Administration: that helping Israel was a solid investment in American security. Underscoring this anti-Soviet theme, the State Department linked the sale of 75 F-16s to Israel that spring to "heightened concerns about the Soviet challenge to the area."[13]

Another change that would affect the debate over closer cooperation with Israel was in the area of domestic politics — or what might be termed domestic realities. In December 1982 the administration had gone to Capitol Hill to request that Congress not approve any increase in aid to Israel. Its failure underscored the deep wellspring of support for Israel, both in Congress and within the American public. By January 1984, according to public opinion polls, Israel had regained all the support lost during the Lebanon War. More telling, the perception of Israel's reliability as an ally compared with America's Arab friends in the region, had been enhanced.[14]

Further, as the 1980s wore on and the number of terrorist incidents increased, the mood of the country was affected by the specter of Arab support for terrorism. This made it even easier for pro-Israel interest groups like AIPAC to find a sympathetic hearing for their efforts on Capitol Hill. AIPAC's influence grew tremendously in the 1980s as it effectively took advantage of changes in lobbying regulations, the dispersal of power in Congress, the increasing importance of grassroots lobbying, and the conservative mood of the country to skillfully present the Israeli case.[15] As mentioned earlier, one aspect of AIPAC's lobbying efforts had become the institutionalization of strategic cooperation.

In the final analysis, the scales for strategic cooperation were tipped by the president himself. With the worst of US-Israel relations behind him, Reagan reverted to his earlier sympathy toward Israel. As a senior administration official (George Shultz, although not identified) said on background in mid-November as the administration was debating closer cooperation with Israel, "Sometimes there are people who disagree with me within the Administration and if I get too frustrated, I just suggest that we have a meeting with the President and see what he has to say, and that settles it."[16]

Opposition to strategic cooperation had not changed significantly from 1981. Defense Secretary Weinberger was still opposed (which meant that, despite pockets of support within the Pentagon, the Defense Department as a whole was opposed), as were parts of the State Department, particularly in the Near East and South Asian (NEA) Bureau. The reasons for opposing strategic cooperation had also remained constant: it would disrupt US interests in the Arab world, thus presenting new opportunities for the Soviets; it would give the Israelis a license to go after US military stocks; it would lead to even greater Israeli demands for aid; it was not necessary, given that practical cooperation had occurred between the two countries for years; and, the complaint heard most frequently in private, it was not "genuine" but "fake," driven by politics.

From the perspective of US military planners, "strategic"

cooperation with Israel probably did not seem to be about genuine strategic interests at all. In their view, abiding US strategic interests lay in Saudi Arabia, or at least in the Arabian Peninsula, where the US required forward positions for protecting the oil fields. Israel was not only geographically not in the right spot, but politically it seemed to have only a spoiler role to play, as events in Lebanon had seemingly proved. Compared with some officials in the State Department who had come around to the view that the US and Israel had mutual interests in Lebanon, the Pentagon's perspective continued to be shaped by the confrontations that had occurred with Israeli forces there and by bitterness over the late 1983 bombing of the Marine barracks, which some people suspected Israeli intelligence had prior warning of.

From this perspective, Israel's policies in late 1983 continued to be provocative enough so as to ensure that any increase in US-Israeli cooperation — even against terrorism — would simply make matters worse with the Arabs. And, with a Marine contingent remaining in Beirut, any closer cooperation with Israel seemed dangerous. As Chairman of the Joint Chiefs John Vessey said in an interview in late 1983 in which he criticized the idea of strategic cooperation with Israel, "We don't need to be siding with either the Israelis or the Syrians in trying to reestablish Lebanon."[17]

But there was one small crack in the Defense Department's opposition to closer cooperation with Israel: the US Navy was looking for a port to support the Sixth Fleet. In mid-November 1983 a US supply ship, the USS Rigel, arrived in Haifa for boiler repairs at the Israel Shipyards.[18] This marked the first time that the Sixth Fleet had sent one of its ships to Israel for major repairs.

Looking at these diverse impulses, it is clear that there was no single factor driving strategic cooperation. When most Israelis involved during this period were asked to explain the administration's turnaround, they pointed to Lebanon and the administration's recognition that lack of cooperation there had seriously undermined US policy. The Americans, when asked the same question, also noted the Lebanon context, but seemed to see strategic cooperation with almost an air of inevitability: the Israelis wanted it and the US wanted closer relations. Given this convergence of interests, it would have occurred sooner or later.

Nearly every player in Washington had his or her own reasons for supporting or opposing strategic cooperation:

— The NSC was for it because it fit in with an increasingly activist approach to the region and it sent a tough message to Moscow. "Strategic," in the NSC view, meant being dealt another card to use in the murky world of dealings and double-dealings against terrorists and other bad guys in the Middle East.

— George Shultz's support for strategic cooperation stemmed from his overall view of US-Israel relations: he admired the Israelis, saw a number of mutual interests between the two countries, and believed that a strong Israel was in America's interest. But he also believed that by making Israel feel more secure, it would be more willing to make concessions for peace. Thus, "strategic" for Shultz probably had a lot to do with maintaining stability in the region and remaining true to a trusted friend.

— Larry Eagleburger, like Kissinger before him, viewed Israel in realpolitik terms; it only made sense for the US to effectively use what resources it had in the struggle against Soviet influence and radical Arab states in the region. "Strategic," in this case, came the closest to a traditional meaning of strategic interests. Israel was strong, reliable and friendly: the US should take advantage of that.

— President Reagan's domestic advisors probably favored strategic cooperation to shore up domestic constituencies before the 1984 election. Reagan, for his part, seemed instinctively to favor closer cooperation (vaguely defined) with Israel and, with the bitter years behind, reverted to his original sympathetic support. "Strategic," in political terms, meant crossing rhetorically from "friend" to "ally."

— Weinberger, and others, opposed strategic cooperation in part because they saw nothing "strategic" about what Israel had to offer. "Strategic" meant oil, mineral resources, Saudi Arabia; Israel was a liability in these terms.

Down to the Wire

In late October 1983, following the killing of 241 American servicemen in a terrorist attack in Beirut, the president approved a directive setting out a tougher policy toward Syria, including use of American firepower against Syrian-controlled sectors of Lebanon.[19] Improving relations with Israel, which after all was a frontline state against Syria, was part of the overall plan. But while the directive must have contained at least a vague reference to cooperation with Israel, it apparently did not include any specific plan for handling strategic cooperation between the two countries.

From the time that the directive was approved by the president until November 28, when newly-appointed Prime Minister Yitzhak Shamir and Defense Minister Arens arrived in Washington, the national security bureaucracy fought over the handling of strategic cooperation with Israel. Second-tier officials from State, Defense, JCS (Joint Chiefs of Staff), CIA and the NSC met in drawn-out sessions that were undoubtedly marked by personal as well as institutional hostility. Since these officials were trying to forge a compromise on an issue that continued to divide their bosses, George Shultz and Caspar Weinberger, it should have come as no surprise that on the eve of Shamir and Arens' arrival in Washington, a final decision had still not been made.

Meanwhile, two Israeli officials who would be instrumental in shaping strategic cooperation, Major General (res.) Menachem (Mendy) Meron (director general of the Ministry of Defense) and Hanon Bar-On (deputy director general of the Foreign Ministry) arrived in Washington to prepare the Shamir visit. They clearly recognized the need for a renewed military-to-military dialogue (which had been cut-off in 1981), if for no other reason than to provide a mechanism to coordinate US military assistance flowing into Israel. But the signals from their contacts were not very promising; one Pentagon official warned them against "Israeli arm-twisting." Thus, even though the Israelis knew the subject of strategic cooperation was under discussion, on the eve of the visit they were still not certain how the issue would be resolved.

According to a senior official involved in this process, the president made his decision about strategic cooperation on the morning of Shamir's visit, on the basis of a "compromise" paper put together by NSC Adviser McFarlane: the administration would make no a priori decisions as to what strategic cooperation would cover; rather, it would create a joint Israeli-American political-military group which would explore areas of overlapping military interests. While this may not have seemed very substantial given the history of strategic cooperation, one subtle but important change was made vis-a-vis the 1981 setup, that would help to ensure its success: control of the joint group was transferred from Defense to the State Department.

The fresh start on strategic cooperation during the Shamir visit of late November 1983 was matched by a more forthcoming American approach to issues across the board. The United States made economic and military concessions to Israel, including permitting the use of US funds for the development of the Lavi combat aircraft, and a commitment to negotiate a free-trade agreement between the two countries. Discussions began on expanding the original 1979 MOA on defense cooperation and trade, of key interest to Israel. Meanwhile, the level of military aid issued in grants, as compared to repayable loans, went up, and the administration declared that it would grant an additional $910 million in economic assistance. Finally, testifying to the US Navy's interest in Haifa, Israel was also promised that the US Sixth Fleet would spend $200 million in Israel.

A Whole New Ballgame

The net result was a remarkably different environment for the agreement on strategic cooperation, compared to 1981. In 1983, cooperation was part of an overall US program to improve relations with Jerusalem, pulling in a much wider community of interests to buttress the agreement — military, political and economic. This, in turn, would help to create an interlocking web of institutional interests across the spectrum of Washington's bureaucracy.

Moreover, the lack of a formal document, which at first glance appeared to reflect the continuing differences within the administration, would turn out to be the most significant advantage of the new understanding on strategic cooperation. The lack of formality served to create parameters for cooperation that were theoretically sky-high. As a result, unprecedented responsibility and influence in fashioning and defining strategic cooperation would fall to the participants involved in the newly-formed joint group.

The 1981 MOU had ultimately broken down over the Reagan Administration's hope that "collateral benefits" would flow from the strategic understanding, particularly in the form of greater consultations about planned Israeli activities. In 1983, concern about Israel's military activities in the region had largely been replaced by interest in a more subtle collateral benefit: that a more confident and secure Israel would also be an Israel more willing to take risks for peace. Administration officials would refer repeatedly to their hopes for drawing a "secure" Israel into the peace process if an Arab interlocutor could be found. This quiet reaffirmation of a linkage between progress on the peace front and a strong Israel supported by firm strategic ties with the US, would have particularly important implications during the Bush Administration.

But the most striking change from 1981 was the overall raison d'etre for strategic cooperation. In 1981, the MOU had defined the objective of strategic cooperation as dealing with threats from the Soviet Union introduced from outside the region. In other words, the rationale was Soviet, but it lacked any concrete context as far as Israel was concerned. In 1983, this Soviet threat was given a name: Syria. In a formal statement at the conclusion of the Shamir visit, Reagan expressed concern with the Soviet presence and arms buildup in Syria, and stated that increased military cooperation with Israel would give priority attention to "the threat to our mutual interests posed by increased Soviet involvement in the Middle East."[20] An administration official subsequently stated that the "message" of strategic cooperation should be heard by both Syria and the USSR.[21]

Behind this US expression of concern about Syria and the Soviet Union was, of course, Lebanon, where US Marines were still entrenched. Senior Israeli and American officials were quoted as emphasizing that a central reason behind the closer coordination between the two countries was to bolster the Lebanese government and to press the Syrians to agree eventually to join Israel in withdrawing troops from Lebanon — which would then allow for an honorable departure of American troops.[22] The perceived key to making this happen was pressure on Syria, through a show of combined US and Israeli strength.

The importance of Lebanon to this equation was underscored by the visit of the Lebanese president to Washington just one day after Shamir had left. Less than a week later, in another demonstration of the more forceful US approach to dealing with the Syrian presence in Lebanon, Washington ordered air strikes on Syrian positions in Lebanon, losing two US planes in the process.

What all this meant for Israel was that it had finally been assigned an important place in the Reagan Administration's strategy for the Middle East region. Mutual interests had been identified, and traditional fears regarding excessive intimacy with Israel had been overcome by those who saw advantages in such an alliance.

While critics would charge that domestic political considerations had driven the whole process, this seems an exaggeration. True, as so often in the past, the administration had to take into account the overwhelming support that Israel could marshal on Capitol Hill. But the final decision to proceed with closer cooperation with Israel was driven by those events in the region that had proved so disappointing to the Reagan Administration, and which now seemed to require a new approach. Just as important in this regard was the existence of a different leadership in Jerusalem that proved willing to work with Washington.

Yet being viewed as an important part of the overall US strategy in the region was one proposition; realizing genuine "strategic cooperation" in the area of defense and security was clearly another. As Israel had seen in the past, American strategies could come and go, and with them, Israel's perceived role at any given time. The real test was still ahead: whether a cooperative relationship would indeed be institutionalized so that, even if the immediate strategy vis-a-vis Syria disappeared, a mandate to promote forms of cooperation between the two countries would live on.

Thus began the second phase of strategic cooperation. In many respects it would prove to be more important than the first, since it would decide the shape and parameters for what was hoped would be a lasting cooperative program. This process would be shaped by different interests and players: its key issues would revolve around issues like resource allocation and the costs and benefits of using specific facilities in Israel. The key players would be almost invisible officials within the bureaucratic structures in both countries; no longer would the concept be batted about by politicians or grand foreign policy strategists. It was, as is often said in America, a whole new ballgame.

Chapter 5. Strategic Cooperation is Finally Defined

No-Nonsense Cooperation

Given the difficulties leading up to strategic cooperation and the fact that Israel possessed little more than a declaration of intentions by the American side, the Israeli team approached the first session of the newly-created Joint Political-Military Group (JPMG) in January 1984 with some uncertainty. Major General (res.) Menachem (Mendy) Meron, director general of the Ministry of Defense, who would lead the Israeli side, had already decided that he would not take the initiative at the meeting but would wait to hear the Americans express their views on the nature of strategic cooperation. After the experience in 1981, he was convinced that both sides must truly desire strategic cooperation if it were to be meaningful.[1]

The US side was led by Rear Admiral Jonathan Howe, then director of Political-Military Affairs at the State Department. Howe was a successful, no-nonsense Navy officer who had a reputation for getting the job done. It was probably due to his military background, energy and intelligence, that he was able to put together and ride herd over a US team that included Defense and JCS officials as well as NSC and Middle East specialists from the State Department's NEA Bureau.

Howe and Meron would set the tone for the JPMG — constructive, collegial and frank. While both officials were used to speaking their minds, they were also disposed toward problem-solving rather than confrontation. Even as the first session got underway, both sides demonstrated their interest in reaching practical agreements that would be of real benefit to their respective countries.

Thus, even as the two sides began to discuss the larger conceptual issues of strategic cooperation, agreement was reached on several joint projects. The first was in the area of military medical programs, where three agreements were quickly concluded in December 1983. The first gave American forces access to Israeli hospitals in the event of another disaster like the truck bombing of the American Marine compound in Beirut in October, or similarly destructive hostilities. The second would permit the US to store medical supplies in Israel for use by American forces as necessary. This marked the first concrete agreement on prepositioning in Israel. Under a third agreement, American and Israeli military doctors would carry out exchange visits.[2]

The conclusion of these agreements in non-controversial fields helped to demonstrate the seriousness with which both sides were approaching strategic cooperation. By June 1984, two joint medical exercises were conducted which simulated the evacuation of US forces from Navy ships to Israeli hospitals.[3] This marked the first time the two countries had engaged in joint exercises involving their military forces.

A second area of practical cooperation that would be decided relatively quickly was the renewal of the 1979 US-Israeli Memorandum of Agreement (MOA) on defense cooperation. Signed on March 19, 1984 by Weinberger and Arens, the MOA was very important to Israel's efforts to maintain an independent military-industrial capacity. Given the small size of Israel's own internal defense market and the political constraints limiting its export opportunities, defense-industrial cooperation with the United States could open the vast US defense market to Israeli systems. There were additional important spin-offs from defense-industrial cooperation, particularly in the area of technology, also considered vital to Israel's long-term military potential.[4] Although this type of cooperation was more technical and diffused in terms of participants, it would become, at least for the Israelis, one of the most important aspects of strategic cooperation.

But What Is Strategic Cooperation?

The most difficult and important issue that the first session of the JPMG would grapple with was to define the parameters for strategic cooperation. In President Reagan's statement announcing the formation of the JPMG, three broad areas of potential cooperation had been listed: combined planning, joint exercises, and requirements for prepositioning of US equipment in Israel.

What was not defined in the president's statement were the contingencies or scenarios under which these activities would occur. Would strategic cooperation be aimed only at countering the Soviets, or at countering their Arab clients as well? Would strategic cooperation encompass threats to the entire region, including the Persian Gulf, or simply the Eastern Mediterranean? These, of course, were the key issues that in 1981 had helped to strip the MOU of much of its significance.

Despite the administration's preoccupation with Syria and Lebanon, the thrust of remarks by American officials emphasized the anti-Soviet nature of the agreement, rather than the Arab angle. In public remarks made as Shamir was departing Washington, President Reagan stated that the JPMG would give priority attention to "the threat to our mutual interest posed by increased Soviet involvement in the Middle East."[5] Speaking on background following the president's remarks, a senior administration official stressed that strategic cooperation was not conceived as a military axis directed against the Arabs.[6] Unnamed Pentagon officials went even further with reporters, arguing that the new venture was "more of an anti-Soviet alliance" than was the case with the 1981 agreement.[7]

In contrast Shamir, in his parting remarks, carefully avoided explicitly linking strategic cooperation to the Soviet threat, stating that the aim was to "strengthen Israel and to deter threats to the region." Shamir's only allusion to the Soviets was an indirect reference to the concentration of Soviet arms and personnel in Syria, which constituted the "major threat to peace in our area." The prime minister had clearly learned a lesson from 1981, when Israel had been burned by explicit references to the Soviet Union. Now the Israelis wished to avoid any unnecessary antagonism with a country with which Israel shared an important historical and cultural background, and which also happened to hold the key to the emigration of 2-3 million Jews.

On the second issue of Israel's role in the region, especially the Gulf, there were also somewhat mixed signals from the American side at the start of the process. The 1981 MOU had deliberately avoided any suggestion that US-Israeli cooperation would be aimed at influencing events in the region or had any utility in the

Gulf context. But at least on the question of prepositioning in Israel, the issue appears to have been revisited in 1983. A senior State Department official, speaking on background in mid-November, was asked whether the United States considered Israel of any importance in helping to maintain stability in the Gulf. His response noted that in view of the distance from Israel to the Gulf, it was not practical to talk about using Israel for such things as flying combat aircraft back and forth, or protecting international waters there. That said, he added: "that doesn't mean that you can't position supplies and things" in Israel.[8]

In the lead-up to the first JPMG in January 1984, administration officials referred to the Gulf in conversations with the press in two separate but related contexts. The first concerned the agreement on prepositioning medical supplies in Israel. According to an administration source, the supplies would be used by American forces if they became engaged in combat near Israel "or around the Persian Gulf."[9] The second had to do with prepositioning weapons and military equipment in Israel; some administration officials said this would ease operations if US CENTCOM (previously the Rapid Deployment Force) was sent to secure oil resources around the Persian Gulf.[10]

Thus all the old issues were back on the table when the first JPMG met on January 23: the Eastern Mediterranean, of course Syria, other Arab threats to Israel, and the Persian Gulf. According to a knowledgeable source, the Israeli side specifically sought to discuss contingencies involving Syrian action in Lebanon or Jordan backed by the USSR, and Persian Gulf contingencies in which Moscow was only in the background.[11] In other words, Israel was interested in scenarios involving hostile actions that could either directly or indirectly affect its security interests and in which the Soviets, based on their historical reticence to become directly involved in Middle East conflicts, would play relatively minor roles. From the Israeli perspective, the point of strategic cooperation should have to deal with the very real Arab capabilities that posed a threat to Israeli security.

The US, however, was not willing to risk appearing to be colluding with Israel against Arab states, even those considered the most radical by Washington. So the American side insisted exclusively on discussing contingencies in which the USSR was the major combatant. This could involve Syria or Lebanon or even Jordan, but the thrust of the threat had to be the Soviet Union itself.[12] From the American perspective, one clear example of this would be a Soviet threat to the Eastern Mediterranean.

By the time of the second JPMG meeting in June 1984, the Israelis had reluctantly agreed to the Soviet-dominated scenarios. Meanwhile, because of strenuous objections from CENTCOM to involving Israel in its theater of operations, even where the Soviets were involved, the Persian Gulf contingency was dropped altogether.[13]

The effect of this was to exclude certain categories of contingencies from the parameters of strategic cooperation. Theoretically, joint planning would not cover a threat to Israel from non-Soviet sources, and there would be no US-Israeli military cooperation in a situation that was not dominated by the Soviet Union. To illustrate what this might mean in practical terms, these parameters would not necessarily provide for the type of US-Israeli cooperation that occurred in 1970 in Jordan. Moreover, all combined planning, joint exercises, and prepositioning would be governed by the agreed Soviet thrust of strategic cooperation.

From the perspective of Yitzhak Rabin, then Israeli defense minister, this situation highlighted the key disadvantage of trying to *formalize* cooperation between the sides: in order to agree on the areas that strategic cooperation would cover, it also required specifying what cooperation could not be used for.[14]

Yet the practical consequences of this disadvantage were, in fact, not very great. First, it is important to realize that there was nothing about strategic cooperation that was either binding, like a defense treaty, or which called for an automatic response on the part of one of the parties. In 1986, Rabin stated in an interview that there was no agreement between the sides on the nature of the circumstances that would result in the conduct of joint military operations.[15] More recently, Defense Minister Arens stated that strategic cooperation "only makes provision for simultaneous engagement if the security of the two parties is threatened."[16] Even then, circumstances would be considered on a case-by-case basis with regard to appropriate action. This gave a large measure of flexibility to both sides during a crisis to respond on the basis of the conditions of the moment. Whether certain scenarios were theoretically ruled out or in, would not necessarily count for much in the heat of the moment.

What would count, however, would be the capabilities that had developed on either side in the course of planning for specific scenarios. Thus, regardless of the rationale governing the two sides' activities, in the event of a crisis Israel and the United States would be better prepared to face whatever enemy came along.[17]

Thus the import of the Soviet-dominated scenarios was threefold. First, they provided an important overall rationale for strategic cooperation that could be used by the Americans to good effect in the Arab world. Secondly, this was a way for both sides to paper over their differences regarding the parameters of strategic cooperation and to move ahead with activities that would result in improved capabilities.

Finally, the scenarios made concrete for the first time a US commitment to deter the Soviet Union vis-a-vis Israel. Such a commitment had been given by Washington, and then taken away, in 1970 during the Jordan crisis; it had been reaffirmed in vague terms in the 1975 MOA. Now, for the first time, a US commitment to Israel (albeit a non-binding one) in the face of the Soviet threat was embodied in planning for specific scenarios. This was good news for Israeli strategic planners; they had long recognized that, in the face of a threat from the Soviet Union, Israel needed deterrent protection from its own superpower mentor, the United States.

Meanwhile, the framework that was in place would cover two types of scenarios: cooperation against a direct Soviet threat to the region, including through an Arab client, and cooperation in the event that the United States was involved with Soviet forces outside the region in a context that might affect Israel — e.g. the Eastern Mediterranean. Inter-Arab issues were deliberately left out of this framework, reflecting traditional sensitivities in Washington. They would be kept completely separate from the Israel track.

This left just one type of scenario that fell outside both the Israel and CENTCOM tracks: a direct threat by an Arab state or states to Israel's security, that was not supported by the Soviet Union.

Despite the longstanding US commitment to Israel's security and the record of US support during the 1973 war, it was generally understood that the American position in the event of another attack would be somewhat scenario-dependent: Was it a clear act of Arab aggression? Was the State of Israel in need of assistance? Were there other extenuating circumstances?

That said, strategic cooperation would go farther than any previous effort in US-Israel relations to ensure that US support would be there for Israel in the event of an Arab attack. Although not often cast in these terms, one consequence of having US and Israeli forces train together is familiarization; in time of crisis, this would facilitate coordination.[18] And what, after all, is the point of prepositioning dual-use ammunition and spare parts in Israel if not for Israel to be able to draw on them in time of crisis? Perhaps a "senior administration official" (clearly George Shultz) said it best just before strategic cooperation was decided in November 1983. Asked about possible prepositioning in Israel, he responded: "We want to try to work out arrangements that do everything we can to help Israel maintain its posture of having an effective military advantage in the region so that it isn't going to be knocked over by somebody's superior military power. *That is sort of the point of all of these things.*"[19]

In other words, leaving aside for the moment the Soviet-dominated scenarios that were believed only to varying degrees by US and Israeli officials, everyone could agree on the commitment to Israel's security. This indeed was the bottom line of strategic cooperation as far as the US was concerned, and it certainly was the aspect that most interested Israel. It thus stands to reason that the "scenario" of providing for Israel's defense would, in the final analysis, become the one constant of strategic cooperation and planning through the years.

Strategic Cooperation Takes on Practical Meaning

With the parameters of strategic cooperation in place, both sides turned their attention to finding practical areas of cooperation. In the course of 1984 many US military leaders traveled to Israel to see what the Israeli military had to offer. Of particular interest was Israel's advanced technological base and its renowned ability quickly and efficiently to translate ideas into new military hardware.

In January 1984 General John W. Vessey Jr. became the first chairman of the Joint Chiefs of Staff to visit Israel. The commandant of the Marine Corps, General P.X. Kelly, followed shortly thereafter and returned, according to Israeli press accounts, a "true believer in the strategic importance of Israel to the US."[20] A new tone was also reflected during a trip to Israel in late 1984 by Defense Minister Weinberger. At the end of what he termed a "most successful visit," Weinberger announced a number of new agreements in the defense area, including the release of US composite technology that was needed by Israel to produce the Lavi combat aircraft. Although he avoided any reference to strategic cooperation between the two countries, he did, at one point, note that he had been struck during his meetings at the Ministry of Defense by "the similarity of our objectives."[21]

Of all the US military services, the US Navy quickly developed the most extensive cooperative relationship with Israel. By mid-April 1985, Secretary of the Navy John Lehman had already made three visits to Israel and was obviously enthused about what he saw there. The Sixth Fleet had become a regular caller at Haifa Port, where the Navy could take advantage of high-quality workmanship at the port's maintenance and repair facilities, its willingness to accept American warships on short notice, and the ready availability of superior-quality fresh food supplies. In addition to these advantages, Haifa was an extremely friendly port for shore leave in that part of the world — a rare commodity indeed by the mid-1980s.

Lehman also was impressed with Israel's innovative defense products and its strong technological base. He foresaw closer cooperation as having important benefits for US naval modernization. During a press conference in Jerusalem in April 1985, Lehman announced agreement on a number of joint development projects of naval systems, including a decision to jointly develop and produce a new naval missile.[22]

Another important aspect of cooperation was Israel's unique

ability to provide realistic training opportunities for US naval forces. Already by 1985, Lehman had arranged to lease and maintain two squadrons of the Israeli Kfir jet, which was similar to the Soviet-built MiG-23, for use in US Navy and Marine aggressor training.[23] The jets were specially equipped by the Israelis for this purpose. Because Israel's diesel submarines shared some characteristics with Warsaw Pact systems and Israeli submariners proved skilled at evasive maneuvers, the US Navy also found it advantageous to engage in anti-submarine warfare exercises with Israel. The US would later take the unusual step of allowing Israel to use US FMS funds to cover part of the costs of purchasing two diesel submarines (which the US does not produce) from Germany to replace its aging Gal-class vessels.

There were also unique training opportunities within Israel itself that all of the US services could take advantage of. Although the Negev desert is small relative to other US training sites, virtually all of it (about 85 percent) can be used for training purposes. In practical terms, this meant that the US could avoid the type of problems that had arisen in Germany as a result of the close proximity of US forces to civilian population and civilian air traffic. The Negev is also home to three important Israeli military airbases, two of which were constructed by the US as compensation for Israeli withdrawal from bases in the Sinai. As Israeli leaders, beginning with Prime Minister Begin had repeatedly emphasized, not only did Israel have such facilities, it was willing to modify them or take any other steps necessary to allow the US military to use them.

In 1986 it was reported that US Sixth Fleet fighter pilots had been practicing precision attacks at a site in the Negev desert since late 1985 at least.[24] Later in the decade, US Army Apache helicopters practised on sophisticated Israeli gunnery ranges in the Negev.[25] Finally, the Marine Corps also discovered unique training opportunities in Israel in the form of live-fire exercises, beach assaults, and even combined-arms exercises. Testifying to both sides' interest in desert training opportunities, Defense Minister Carlucci was taken to the Negev during his visit to Israel in November 1988 to observe an Israeli exercise posing Israeli-built Merkava tanks against American-made M-60s.[26]

Meanwhile, plans were slowly moving ahead on prepositioning arrangements that would require the construction or utilization of Israeli facilities. In July 1986 the Israeli press reported that the 1987 US Military Construction Bill authorized approximately $70 million for prepositioning war materiel in Israel for use by US armed forces in times of crisis.[27] An earlier report in March had specified that ammunition would be stored in new bunkers.[28] In April 1987 it was further reported that not only prepositioning but also the construction of a US Air Force hospital in Israel were under discussion by the JPMG.[29]

All of this contributed to a completely different environment for the defense dialogue between the two countries. As Ambassador Lewis said in 1985, "I can honestly say that the level of cooperation is now at an unprecedented level. Today, unlike some time past, when an Israeli defense minister goes to Washington, he doesn't have a long list of issues on which he must try to persuade skeptical American officials that the value of Israeli cooperation and in the military field warrants more generous treatment. That kind of visit is in the past."[30]

Muted Opposition

It would be wrong to conclude from these developments that earlier opposition to strategic cooperation with Israel had simply evaporated. Rather, as implementation of the program got underway, two important reasons for opposing closer cooperation seemed to diminish, thereby muting residual opposition.

First, as a result of a change in Israeli leadership, Israel's regional policies, particularly regarding the peace process, became more to Washington's liking. It was no coincidence that Weinberger's late 1984 remarks about common objectives came after the appointment of Labor Party leader Shimon Peres as prime minister. Peres' two-year stint in office would consolidate US-Israel relations like no other period before, largely because of the cooperative working relationship that developed and the similar identification of objectives between Jerusalem and Washington. What the new Israeli government and attitude to peace meant for Weinberger was a reduced risk that closer identification with

Israel would negatively affect US interests in the Arab world.

Secondly, the much-feared reaction from the Arab states to closer cooperation with Israel never materialized. Indeed, as time went on, it appeared that the administration had finally found a way to realize Alexander Haig's original goal of conducting serious military cooperation with both Israel and the Arab states. Although there was some criticism from several Arab capitals immediately following the 1983 announcement of strategic cooperation, the reaction from Egypt was most telling. Following meetings at the State Department, the Egyptian foreign minister expressed satisfaction with assurances he had received, according to which US-Israeli strategic cooperation would not prejudice friendly US ties with the Arabs or US efforts to find peace in the region.[31]

To some extent, the muted Arab reaction simply stemmed from resignation about the US-Israeli relationship. From the Arab perspective, collaboration that comprised military cooperation between Israel and the US had become a fact of life. The concept of strategic cooperation had become part of the region's political landscape.

However, the US could not keep everyone happy without a price. Egypt's reaction was attributable in part to its expectation that, if aid to Israel were to go up or become more concessionary, Egypt would receive proportionately the same benefits, as aid programs to Israel and to Egypt had been linked since Camp David. Secondly, the US now undertook to enhance its relationships with Arab states such as Bahrain, Kuwait, Saudi Arabia, Oman and Jordan. While this did not involve large amounts of aid, it did take the form of contingency planning, exercises and other aspects of military cooperation. Indeed, by early 1987 such cooperation had evolved to the point where the US was willing to commit itself to a reflagging escort regime — Operation "Earnest Will" — at Arab behest.

But if these two concerns about strategic cooperation — which were both related to the Arab reaction — had diminished, there remained charges by some quarters in the administration that strategic cooperation was not "genuine." While collaboration clearly involved practical benefits, doubters charged that it was not driven by strategic imperatives on the US side, but rather by political imperatives, and that basically the entire concept was hyped by overzealous supporters of Israel. It is interesting to note that Caspar Weinberger, writing some years later of his years in the Pentagon, does not refer even once to strategic cooperation with Israel in his book.[32]

Residual concern also remained among the professional military that Israel would be allowed to dip into US equipment stocks; this could mean less for US forces. Because Israel clearly had an "inside track" on Capitol Hill, the US military often felt outgunned and outmaneuvered in the political arena. This naturally gave rise to a certain degree of resentment and a perception that Israel was getting special treatment. There were also institutional biases against strategic cooperation from those parts of the US military charged with defending US interests in the Persian Gulf, such as CENTCOM.

Meanwhile, concern was growing among professional diplomats that US policy in the Middle East was becoming too one-sided, thereby reducing American effectiveness as a mediator between the parties. Particularly as it became increasingly difficult to get approval from Congress for arms packages to Jordan and Saudi Arabia in 1985 and 1986, there were heightened warnings from Assistant Secretary of State for Near East Asia Affairs Richard Murphy, that the US had moved away from its longstanding policy of "even-handedness."[33]

While these concerns were real, the administration's policy of support for Israel did not leave much room for open disagreement. By 1986, US opinion polls reported that the public was more sympathetic to Israel than to the Arab states by a margin of 62 to 13 percent — the largest in four years of asking the question.[34] In the face of such overwhelming support for Israel both in and out of the administration, what had once been clear opposition to strategic cooperation simply became, in the second half of the Reagan Administration, a soft belly of cynicism and skepticism regarding the value of the program.

One event that would greatly add to this underlying cynicism was the arrest in late 1985 of Jonathan Pollard, a civilian analyst for the US Navy, and his subsequent conviction for passing classified documents to Israel. Prime Minister Peres' handling of the affair, including his decision to issue an apology to the United States, helped contain the damage to the US-Israeli relationship. But just below the surface, American officialdom and the general public felt betrayed and shocked, particularly as reports surfaced that Pollard had not been acting in isolation.

The incident also exposed a deeper sense of unease by people both in and out of the administration that the accepted barriers between the two governments had become porous. This perception spawned a number of press articles following the Pollard affair which, citing unnamed administration sources, claimed that Israeli officials had access to top-secret US policy deliberations and knew stock numbers and specifications of new weapons systems even before they were delivered to American armed forces.[35] There were also renewed public warnings that US policy in the region was being distorted by the unusually close relations with Israel. One of these came from Harold Saunders, assistant secretary of state during the Carter Administration, who said that a "cancer was growing" on the US-Israeli relationship and that Israel was enjoying a "virtual blank check."[36]

Such concern only grew with the exposure of the Iran-Contra Affair in late 1986. Although criticism was directed primarily toward the Reagan Administration, Israel's role in the affair was seen by some as one more example of the drawbacks of maintaining too close a relationship with Jerusalem.

The Human Factor

Still, a momentum had developed behind strategic cooperation that far outweighed any misgivings. This was due not only to support from the president and secretary of state, but also to key mid-level officials in both the Defense and State Departments who were unusually adept at manipulating the bureaucratic machinery. The type of institutionalized relationship that developed in just a few short years would not have been possible had there not been highly-motivated officials to initiate and follow through on new ideas, and to come up with creative sources of funding for new projects. Suggestions originally made by Prime Minister Begin and rejected in the early 1980s now found a sympathetic hearing from the JPMG, which was charged with judging such ideas on the basis of merit and practical benefits.

As cooperative projects increased, so too did the number of US officials involved with and exposed to Israel. This was particularly important for the US military which, historically, had had little contact with Israel. While difficult to quantify, this exposure contributed to greater understanding of Israel's problems and, in some cases, a genuine appreciation for strategic cooperation, as the following story illustrates.

In 1984, as the JPMG was getting organized, a military-to-military group was established to direct the day-to-day workings of the new cooperative projects. Control of the group on the American side fell to a submarine officer assigned to the Joint Chiefs of Staff (JCS). At that time, the JCS had had no prior dialogue with the IDF and was still a most skeptical participant in the strategic cooperation program. But despite both this institutional bias and the complete lack of any prior exposure to Israel, the JCS officer in charge of the military group, Admiral Jack Darby, became one of the most genuinely enthusiastic proponents of closer cooperation with Israel. This occurred, as it would for many other unnamed officers, through Darby's personal experiences with Israel, including his visits there.

As with most everything else surrounding strategic cooperation, Darby was invisible to most of the outside world. It was thus fitting that, following his death in the late 1980s, an Israeli plaque dedicated to his role in strategic cooperation would appear without fanfare or publicity in a forest in the Carmel Mountains.[37] It would stand as testimony to the quiet relationship that had built up between many such individuals on both sides.

Strategic Cooperation At the End of The Reagan Era

In 1986, George Shultz reportedly told AIPAC Director Tom Dine that he felt so strongly about Israel's strategic importance that he wanted to "build institutional arrangements so that...if there is a [future] Secretary of State who is not positive about Israel, he will not be able to overcome the bureaucratic relationship between Israel and the US that we have established."[38]

By all appearances, this had been accomplished by the end of the Reagan Administration. A close dialogue had become the norm for relations. Aid had risen to a hefty $3 billion annually, all in grants, and was supplemented by millions more from special arrangements. The free-trade agreement, the first of its kind negotiated by the United States, would usher in a significant increase in joint commerce by eliminating tariffs between the two countries. And underpinning everything was an administration that appeared truly to believe in the special relationship between the two countries. As Tom Dine noted in 1986, there were sympathetic officials at every level of the American government.[39]

An additional codification of the relationship occurred on April 21, 1988, when a Memorandum of Agreement on US-Israeli strategic cooperation was signed by President Reagan and Yitzhak Rabin (see Appendix 2). While it did not spell out in detail all of the areas of ongoing cooperation in the defense field, it made clear that the legacy left for the next administration was a powerful one:

First, the institutionalization of the dialogue had created a self-perpetuating mechanism in support of strategic cooperation:

— The Joint Political-Military Group (JPMG) was meeting biannually to oversee the overall direction of the program and to consider new ideas for cooperative ventures.
— A military-to-military group was meeting more frequently to ensure effective implementation of ongoing projects. This had the added effect of bringing US and Israeli professional military representatives together on a regular basis.
— The Joint Security Assistance Planning Group (JSAP) met annually to discuss the size of Israel's aid package, which only then went to Congress for approval. As one US official noted, "We negotiate everything with them. We don't do that with anyone else."[40]
— And one last group, the Joint Economic Development Group (JEDG), was established in 1985 to discuss Israel's economic problems and to oversee reform efforts.

Secondly, there were now examples of military cooperation with Israel involving all four American services:

- All of the services to varying degrees were taking advantage of Israel's facilities to carry out training exercises, including use of live-fire.
- There were joint air and sea exercises, and there was also extensive use by the US Navy of Israel's port facilities.
- Prepositioning of some US materiel in Israel was moving ahead.
- Finally, both sides had drawn up joint plans, for the first time, to deal with possible scenarios that might affect their security interests.

Third, many genuine examples now existed of US-Israeli partnership in the area of research and technology. Testifying to its demonstrated ability to contribute in this area, Israel was designated a "major, non-NATO ally" by the US Congress in 1987 for purposes of cooperative research and development projects:

- The most visible instance had begun in 1986, when Israel became the third country to join the United States in the SDI program. In 1988, testifying to the success of the program in Israel, agreement was reached on a cooperative SDI project — the Arrow anti-tactical ballistic missile system. The US agreed to pick up 80 percent of R&D costs for phase I.
- By 1988, the US and Israel were cooperating in a variety of weapons development and production projects including aircraft, mini-RPVs, electronics, naval vessels, tank guns, and terminal guidance bombs.[41]
- Because US weapons systems were often used in combat for the first time by Israel and often against Soviet-made weapons, Israel had an important if not necessarily desirable longstanding role to play in the area of weapons evaluation.

Fourth, a web of cooperative arrangements was put in place that greatly facilitated defense trade between the two countries. US purchases of military goods and services from Israel, which were only $9 million in 1983, grew to $240 million in 1987 and were expected to total $480 million in 1988. One example of such sales was the US purchase of Israel's Popeye stand-off air-to-ground missile (now redesignated "Have Nap" or AGM-142).[42]

Finally, the entire relationship was buttressed by an American declaratory policy that openly embraced Israel as an "ally" and which underscored time and again the US commitment to ensuring Israel's security. This rhetorical policy was as important as the concrete measures listed above since it went to the heart of American intentions toward Israel, and stood in sharp contrast to US policy less than a decade before.

Countering the Soviet threat remained the primary justification for strategic cooperation. Yet the nature of Israel's contribution toward that goal was less clear. The Persian Gulf was effectively considered off-limits to US-Israeli cooperation because of strenuous objections from CENTCOM. Cooperation against other Arab states was considered too risky because of US interests in the Arab world. Even the original 1983 emphasis on Syria disappeared over the years. The Eastern Mediterranean remained the one area used by the US to explain Israel's strategic value in practical, military terms.

In 1987, US Assistant Secretary of Defense Richard Armitage was asked what he thought about the assertion that Israel was a strategic liability. His response was to reject the assertion and to note that strategic cooperation was "directed primarily at the Soviet threat in the Eastern Mediterranean."[43] Former Ambassador Sam Lewis noted in 1986 that Israel had become much more important to US strategic thinking — although "hardly central" — because of the potential contribution that Israel could make to US strategic interests in the Eastern Mediterranean.[44] Then-Vice President Bush noted in 1988 that joint planning was underway on "mutual threats in the Mediterranean."[45]

Israel's actual contribution in the Eastern Mediterranean was probably viewed by US military planners as useful but not absolutely essential. Any conflict in that arena would likely be a naval battle with air assets employed. While Israel clearly has capabilities that might be useful in such a scenario, the US Navy has spent billions of dollars to ensure its ability to act autonomously in crisis situations. What the Navy would nevertheless still require are maintenance, repair facilities and shore privileges — all of which are important and which Israel is uniquely situated to provide.

Did all of this add up to a genuine rationale for strategic cooperation? If one were simply looking at Israel's role in US planning against the Soviet Union, probably not. Where US officials always referred to Saudi Arabia's cooperation in defending the Gulf as "essential," Israel's contribution was at most described as "helpful." This obviously was not reflective of Saudi Arabia's greater military prowess; rather, it constituted a hard-nosed assessment of the type of assistance the US would require in the event of a crisis. American scenarios for the Gulf have always had to plan for a conflict — like the 1991 Gulf War — that would require the deployment of US ground troops. This requires not only a friendly host country but an enormous support infrastructure on the ground. At least for now, there would seem to be no comparable scenario or requirements involving the Eastern Mediterranean.

But the legitimacy of US-Israeli strategic cooperation had never been based, from Washington's perspective, on narrow military considerations. Rather, it involved broader US priorities and objectives in the region, including countering the Soviet presence there and convincing Israel's Arab neighbors to be more cooperative. Most importantly, strategic cooperation and all of its constituent components reflected the US commitment to Israel's security. This was based not only on a strong domestic constituency supporting Israel but also on very real strategic considerations about how a weak or defeated Israel would affect strategic stability in the region.

Finally, the Reagan Administration's commitment to strategic cooperation reflected the belief that the only way to make progress on the peace front was through a strong and confident Israel, secure in the friendship of the United States and consequently willing to take risks for peace. While this theme was struck many times by administration officials, one of its clearest expressions came in a White House statement marking the signing of the MOA on strategic cooperation in April 1988. Specifically, the statement read:

> Strategic cooperation can only succeed when there are shared interests, including the commitment to building peace and stability in the region. It reflects the enduring US commitment to Israel's security. That commitment will never flag. The US commitment to peace will also not flag. The President knows that a strong Israel is necessary if peace

is to be possible. He also knows that Israel can never be truly secure without peace.[46]

While George Shultz would set the stage for the new US approach to the peace process and to a US dialogue with the PLO, it would be left to the Bush Administration to more completely explore the relationship between security and peace.

Chapter 6. The Bush Administration

Upon the advent of the Bush Administration, it might have been thought that strategic cooperation would simply be a continuation of the previous eight years under the Reagan Administration. President Bush's rhetorical record was strongly supportive of Israel and of acknowledging Israel's importance to the United States. Meanwhile, the program itself was running smoothly, involved practical benefits for both sides, and had not incurred any significant political costs in the Arab world. It had indeed become, as George Shultz had hoped, institutionalized to the point where it no longer seemed either controversial or daring.

But US-Israeli strategic cooperation would be severely tested under Bush. First, with the passing of the Cold War and the lessening of the Soviet threat, serious questions would be raised as to the rationale of strategic cooperation. Secondly, in the wake of the new administration's efforts on the peace front and the resultant tensions in US-Israel relations, there would be a natural focus on the question of where strategic cooperation fit into broader American policy toward Israel. Was it something that could be used to bring pressure to bear against Israel, or should it be insulated from problems in the relationship? Finally, the Gulf War would provide the most important test of the meaning of the strategic alliance since the concept was first embraced by Ronald Reagan and Menachem Begin in 1981. What was the US commitment to Israel and what did Israel's part of the bargain consist of?

The End of the Cold War

As the decade of the 1980s came to a close, the US stood at the edge of a full-scale revolution in its thinking on foreign policy. For over 40 years the major lines of US foreign policy had been guided and shaped by the specter of Soviet communism. "Containment" was not simply a description of US objectives toward the Soviet Union, but a framework which helped to underpin and justify the whole of US actions around the globe. From fear of internal subversion at home to concern about military defeat abroad, America was preoccupied and haunted by the communist threat.

The disintegration of the Soviet empire and the exposure of systemic weaknesses throughout Soviet communist society stripped America of these obsessions, leaving great uncertainty in their wake. What should America's role in the world be in the absence of a robust and clearly-defined antagonist? What should replace containment of a now visibly weakened Soviet Union? Although the Bush Administration initially tried to argue that the Soviet threat was not gone and that tension could be renewed at any time, it was largely unsuccessful in holding back increasing demands for a "peace dividend" that would be generated by reducing the American military budget.

No aspect of American security policies was spared from the national effort to reassess US strategic priorities and commitments abroad. Plans for cutting back US troops overseas threatened longstanding security arrangements and basing agreements from Europe to Seoul to Manila. After years of viewing Pakistan as a key ally against Soviet encroachment in Southwest Asia, the US rediscovered Pakistan's faults following the Soviet withdrawal from Afghanistan. Even that vaunted symbol of US readiness to engage in war with the Soviet Union — the continuous flights by Air Force "doomsday" planes equipped to direct a nuclear war after a Soviet attack on the US — was sacrificed in July 1990 to the budget squeeze and the superpower thaw. Everywhere one turned, US policymakers seemed to face the dilemma of finding new rationales for old arrangements.

US-Israeli strategic cooperation was no exception. From the outset of the Reagan Administration's interest in strategic cooperation with Israel, it had been couched in terms of heightened US concern over the Soviet threat to the region. The entire premise of the 1981 MOU was the Soviet threat. In 1983 as well, President Reagan had linked strategic cooperation to increased Soviet involvement in the Middle East. This had remained the official US line on strategic cooperation in subsequent years, whenever such an explanation was called for.

It thus should have come as no surprise that, as US-Israel relations soured in late 1989 and 1990, the primary reason offered for the downturn was Israel's reduced importance to the United States in the wake of the diminished Soviet threat. This rationale was repeated so frequently that it appeared to take on an aura of cold hard fact. From a *Washington Post* headline proclaiming that "an anxious Israel" feared that the US was losing interest in it, to other journals predicting the diminution of Israel's value as a strategic asset, commentators and experts in both Israel and the United States were quick to predict the decline of America's interest in Israel.[1]

This handwringing over Israel's strategic value was, to some extent, self-serving, as some Israelis sought to divert attention away from the stalemated peace process, by hinting that Washington was more likely to pressure Israel only because the latter had lost its strategic value. For instance, *Ma'ariv* Editor Ido Dissentshik, appearing on *Nightline* in March 1990, was asked by Ted Koppel about US pressure on Shamir to implement his Palestinian election plan. Without even touching on the accumulated history of the peace process or the pressures that had built-up on both governments on this issue, Dissentshik responded that changes in the world had made Israel less important to the United States. The purported strategic value or lack of value of Israel had become a good "soundbite."

But in Israel the concern expressed over the country's strategic value also reflected serious and genuine fears about the US-Israeli relationship. Many Israelis, even if they believed that US-Israel relations were grounded first and foremost on shared traditions and values, felt more comfortable knowing that there was also a strategic rationale buttressing the relationship. It was a point of pride for Israelis to know that they had an important contribution to make to western security, as well as added insurance that US aid would continue to flow. If this importance had now lessened, it raised disturbing questions about the future US-Israeli relationship.

Israelis on the far right of the political spectrum took this logic one step further, believing that Israel's strategic value was so important that it outweighed all other considerations in the US-Israeli relationship. The US provision of $3 billion in aid to Israel every year reflected the real and significant contribution made by Israel to US security interests. From this perspective, even if the US strongly objected to certain Israeli policies, it could not take any serious punitive measures without damaging its own strategic interests. For these people, the possibility that Israel no longer was perceived as having strategic importance for America meant that not only was there now no basis for US aid and assistance, but there was also nothing keeping the US from exerting intense pressure on Israeli policies on the peace front.

Early Administration Support for Strategic Cooperation

Was there any basis for these concerns? Clearly, US alliance strategy had to be rethought if the need for alliances that contained the Soviet Union had disappeared. Whether "allies" needed "enemies" was a question being asked by strategists around the world, particularly regarding the future of NATO. Assuming the most sweeping scenario, if the US had no need to deploy its forces overseas or no interests to defend abroad, it certainly had no need for the cooperative defense arrangements that had been established around the globe.

But in 1989 and 1990, the United States government seemed more preoccupied with holding the line than with moving to jettison longstanding relationships. First, the Bush Administration stressed time and again that the Soviet threat, while diminished, was still present and could reemerge in the future. Secondly, the administration lost no time in articulating its view of non-Soviet threats to US interests, and the resultant need for highly mobile and lethal US forces capable of intervening and sustaining operations far from home. Third, as the administration struggled with demands to reduce defense spending, opportunities to exploit cooperative research and development programs with other friendly countries refocused attention on the benefits of far-flung alliances.

The implications for Israel of this early effort by the Bush Administration to come to grips with the new defense environment appeared mixed but generally positive. The biggest potential danger for Israel seemed to stem from the intense pressures on the US budget: Israel absorbed some 35 percent of the administration's fiscal 1991 request for security assistance; this was not an easy figure to overlook for US budget planners. The greatest potential benefit from the changes taking place was probably in the area of cooperative research, development and coproduction, where Israel was a proven partner. In addition, if US strategy was moving in the direction of greater reliance on local forces to preserve regional stability, Israel could conceivably assume even greater importance in US calculations and planning for the Middle East.[2] Until actual decisions were made on future defense plans, the only intentions that one could try to gauge with any certainty derived from administration statements about strategic cooperation. And here, indications from the Bush Administration seemed to suggest that even in the wake of the dramatic changes taking place, there still would be a role for strategic cooperation with Israel.

In March 1990, Secretary of Defense Cheney gave a speech to the United Jewish Appeal that directly refuted press speculation that Israel's value had decreased in the wake of improved US-Soviet relations. Cheney declared that America's "bedrock commitment to Israel's security is absolutely unshakable" and affirmed that "we have had and always will have a special relationship with Israel." To make his point, he described the many mutual benefits that had resulted from US-Israeli strategic cooperation, and emphasized the successful continuation of the program during the Bush Administration. Cheney noted that similar concerns about the ending of the Cold War were being expressed in other countries as well, and he emphasized that the dramatic changes occurring in the world made it all the more important to maintain the strength of relationships with American allies.[3]

Discussing the Gulf crisis at the end of 1990, Under Secretary of Defense Paul Wolfowitz went even further in denigrating any negative linkage between Israel's strategic value and the diminished Soviet threat:

> I've heard a lot of nonsense over the last few months about how this crisis demonstrates that with the end of the Cold War, with the Soviet Union gone as a significant threat, that we no longer need strategic cooperation with Israel. First of all, I would say that any particular crisis only proves what's relevant to that crisis, and as someone said, history has more

imagination than the people who write scenarios for us. There have been regional crises in the past in which the Soviet Union had no role to play where Israel played a crucial role in preserving stability; there may be some in the future.[4]

While at least some US officials would no doubt take issue with this characterization of Israel's role in the region, it nevertheless made a very telling point from an insider's perspective about the relative importance, or unimportance, of the Soviet threat for strategic cooperation.

Meanwhile, the strategic cooperation program itself appeared to be prospering under the Bush Administration. As Defense Minister Rabin noted in an interview during Bush's first year, the US was moving ahead on framework agreements that would "institutionalize many of the aspects of cooperation between the defense systems of our two countries."[5] Already in September 1989, a new agreement was signed that allowed the administration for the first time to "lend" materials, supplies and equipment to Israel for military research and development.[6]

Of even greater importance, it was reported that Cheney had decided "in principle" to allow the prepositioning of military equipment that would be suitable for, and could be used by, either US or Israeli forces.[7] In the event of emergency, Israel could draw on the stocks on a cash-and-carry basis; in the meantime, Israel could allow certain categories of its own weapons and ammunition to be reduced to below-normal levels of inventory. This would not only save the IDF money, it would significantly lessen the time required for any US resupply of Israeli forces in time of crisis.[8]

Without a doubt, this was an important step for the US and another signal as to the direction that implementation of strategic cooperation was taking. In the early 1980s, when various groups were pushing for strategic cooperation with Israel, the reasons for prepositioning stocks there were, without exception, related to cutting US deployment times in the event of a Soviet-inspired attack in the Persian Gulf.[9] There was no discussion of the need for "dual-use" arrangements because the point of prepositioning was to better enable the US to defend the region against Soviet aggression. The US decision in 1989 to allow Israel access to the prepositioned stocks indicated that another important objective of prepositioning was now to help Israel defend itself against aggression.

Other elements of strategic cooperation were also expanding. Addressing a group of senior US military officers in September 1989, Israeli Defense Minister Rabin discussed the success of the program, noting that the US and Israel had conducted at least 27 or 28 combined exercises in recent years. He also revealed that US Marine training exercises in Israel involving artillery, live ammunition and attack helicopters had recently been held for the first time at the battalion-level. Rabin noted that the demand was to have more of this type of training in Israel, involving the US Air Force, Navy and Army as well, and that Israel was more than ready to assist.[10]

Rabin visited the US again in January 1990 amid reports that top Pentagon officials desired to strengthen various ongoing projects with Israel — including prepositioning (referred to above), the expansion of joint exercises and training programs, and the continuation of military research and development contracts. Besides meeting with Defense Secretary Cheney, Rabin participated in a round-table discussion on the future of strategic cooperation with senior White House, State Department and Defense officials, including the US secretaries of the Army, Navy and Air Force.[11]

Under Secretary of Defense Paul Wolfowitz returned the visit later that month and reportedly negotiated with Rabin key details of the sale of US Patriot missiles to Israel.[12] The decision to transfer the system (which was originally dedicated to air defense but which later would also be given anti-tactical ballistic missile capability) to Israel marked the first time it would be deployed outside the United States, Japan and NATO.[13] Because the system's activation would eventually be linked to US early-warning satellites, it came to mark an even further deepening of the US-Israeli strategic relationship. It was also yet another indication of the role of strategic cooperation in helping to ensure Israel's defense.

On a much smaller scale, but underscoring the uniqueness of strategic cooperation with Israel, was a decision in August 1989 by the American United Services Organization (USO) to make its Fleet Center in Haifa into the southern anchor of its Mediterranean operation. The previous February the USO had decided, due to budget problems, to close the Center along with 10 others in Mediterranean countries. Testifying to the popularity of Haifa Port for Sixth Fleet sailors, the US Navy weighed in against the decision. Meanwhile, the USO received 200 protest letters against the decision, primarily from American-Jewish circles, which were backed up by some $60,000 raised in support of the center.[14] Only in Israel.

All in all, strategic cooperation not only seemed to be prospering but, for the first time, some US defense officials actually appeared to support the endeavor. Defense Minister Cheney closed his speech to the UJA with a theme often heard during the Reagan Administration: that strategic cooperation was a two-way relationship from which both sides benefited.[15] As further testimony to the roots that strategic cooperation had put down, a conference was held in Washington at the end of March 1990 on defense cooperation between the two countries. Under Secretary Robert Atwood addressed the group, while Air Force General Monahan, who was in charge of the SDI program, reported on the many joint projects between Israel and the US, whereby Israel had become the largest overseas recipient of SDI contracts. And the commander of the Marine Airborne Division, General Pittman, said that "cooperation with Israel is the key to our success in numerous fields."[16]

A New Political Context for Strategic Cooperation

If there was a threat to strategic cooperation, it thus did not appear to come from a traditional source of opposition to the program — military planners charged with ensuring America's security. Although the full effects of budget cutbacks were yet to be felt, the Pentagon did not seem to be spearheading any campaign against strategic cooperation as a whole. US security interests and objectives abroad were still too uncertain and the program, even if not essential for US forces, was definitely yielding concrete advantages for certain sectors. Moreover, Defense Secretary Cheney seemed to have none of Secretary Weinberger's biases against Israel.

Any change in the way the administration viewed strategic cooperation was thus a subtle one, related to Washington's political strategy in the region and to the goals that policymakers wanted from the strategic relationship with Israel. Just as the major impetus for strategic cooperation in 1983 had come from political-military strategists (with the emphasis on political) at the State Department and the NSC, so too did it stand to reason that any readjustment in strategic cooperation would also come from those officials charged with crafting overall US strategy in the region.

In 1983, as described in the previous section, strategic cooperation was conceived as part of a broader US strategy aimed at countering Soviet influence, particularly in Syria, and thereby creating new options vis-a-vis the Arab countries. Like Kissinger's strategy in the early 1970s, the key US card was the American relationship with Israel. Following US efforts to strengthen relations with Israel in the early 1970s, one by-product had indeed been the creation of dramatic new options with Egypt and in the region as a whole.

The repeat of this grand strategy in the 1980s likewise had had some successes. Compared with the Arab lack of willingness to cooperate with US objectives in the region in the mid-1980s that had frustrated George Shultz, new opportunities seemed to be emerging. This in no small part was due to the weakened Soviet position in the region and the new Soviet posture toward the Arab-Israel conflict, which raised the possibility in Washington for the first time that Moscow might be a partner rather than an obstacle to peace.

Meanwhile, the price of ignoring possible new opportunities was also perceived to be high by Washington: the Palestinian uprising in the Israeli Occupied Territories — the intifada — which had begun in 1987, showed no signs of abating, and was gradually eroding Israel's image in the United States. Also, the region as a whole appeared to be on the brink of spinning out of control with the proliferation of missiles and nonconventional weaponry.

Thus in the broadest sense US strategic priorities had indeed undergone change in the wake of the ending of the Cold War. This had nothing to do with whether the US required access to more facilities in Israel or desired training opportunities with Israeli forces. It had everything to do with perceived new opportunities that had developed in the region. Not that Israel was no longer important to the US — it continued to provide a key source of influence in the region. But US strategy had never been to build up a strong alliance with Israel and then simply sit on that status quo. The point was to use the new conditions that resulted from this policy — in this case, a strong, confident Israel that could take "risks for peace" and a new willingness on the part of the Arab states to cooperate — to work toward the abiding American interest of finding a settlement to the Arab-Israeli dispute.

The relationship between strength and peace had been a pervasive theme in US policies since at least the 1970s. The Reagan Administration had sought to establish a subtle but clear linkage between strategic cooperation and peace which, in turn, was passed onto the next administration. By the beginning of the Bush presidency it seemed clear that, from the American perspective, the time had arrived to test the thesis of peace on the basis of strength.

Newly-appointed Secretary of State James Baker lost no time in articulating the new US emphasis on peace in a speech to AIPAC on May 22, 1989.[17] He began by lauding the groundwork that had been laid during the Reagan years in giving "fiber and sinew" to the US-Israeli strategic relationship. Baker then used the rest of the speech to clearly lay-out the Bush Administration's belief that the time had arrived to use this strengthened relationship to move on the abiding American and Israeli objective of finding a peaceful settlement to the problems of the region.

Baker's AIPAC speech, and indeed the entire Bush emphasis on finding a settlement with the Palestinians, came as a rude awakening to the Shamir government. Under the best of conditions, any concerted effort to work toward peace in the region was bound to lead to genuine, perhaps unbridgeable differences between the US and Israel. The issues, after all, touched on questions and fears that went to the heart of Israel's existence as a nation. A difficult situation was soon to become worse, however, because of mistakes that would be made on both sides, the personal hostility that developed between the leaders of both countries, and a mutual lack of trust and confidence.

In the course of 1989 and 1990, event after event contributed to the downward spiral of relations: the Israeli decision to build new settlements after President Bush believed that he had been given a pledge by Shamir to cease further settlements; Shamir's statement in early 1990 about the need for a "big Israel" to settle the massive new waves of Jewish immigrants from the Soviet Union, and Bush's statement a month later opposing further settlement activity in Jerusalem; the breakdown of US efforts to get an Israeli-Palestinian dialogue started and the subsequent collapse of the Israeli unity government over the issue; the Israeli government's covert sponsorship of a Jewish settlement in the Christian quarter of Jerusalem, which was denounced even by AIPAC; and the eventual formation of a narrow right-wing government in Israel that seemed to portend even greater confrontations between Washington and Jerusalem.

By the summer of 1990, the message that visitors from Washington were bringing to Israel was that relations were not far from crisis point. Frustration with Israeli policies and a perception that Israel was the obstacle to peace had spread even to Capitol Hill.[18] Lawmakers there were under intense budgetary pressure to come up with new funds to support the fledgling democracies in Eastern Europe as well as in Nicaragua and in Panama. Compared with the dramatic developments occurring all over the world, the Israeli leadership appeared out-of-step and mired in old thinking. It was only a matter of time before US financial aid to Israel and US frustration with Israel would be quietly discussed as two sides of the same coin.

In January 1990 Senator Robert Dole proposed, apparently at the request of the administration, an across-the-board, five percent reduction in assistance to the five major recipients of US aid, including Israel.[19] Although Congress proved unwilling to support the proposal, the word spread that a number of congressmen privately favored the idea. By the time the wrangling began over Israel's request for a $400 million housing loan guarantee, it became clear that some support did indeed exist for linkage, however subtle, between US aid and Israel's position on issues related to peace. In a largely symbolic act, Congress imposed a $1.8 million fee on the housing loan which corresponded to the amount of aid provided by the Israeli government to the Jewish settlement in Jerusalem's Christian Quarter.[20]

As the Reagan years had demonstrated, strategic cooperation was not simply about practical benefits but about a grander sense of alliance between the two states that rested foremost on perceived mutual interests, and which was supported by a rhetorical embrace that declared Israel an "ally." The net effect of events in 1989 and 1990 was to cast doubt on this larger sense of partnership. Perceived mutual interests had given way to intense differences over the peace process. The rhetorical embrace of earlier years turned cool as President Bush avoided personal contact with the Israeli prime minister. While this may have started as a tactic to bring pressure to bear on Israel, by the summer of 1990 it loomed as a potentially important piece of the strategic equation.

Thus, on the eve of Iraq's invasion of Kuwait, there was a perception of crisis in the US-Israeli relationship, and fear that differences between the two countries might simply be too wide to bridge. Although strategic cooperation per se appeared to be flourishing, it was not clear how it would weather a genuine downturn in bilateral relations. Without doing away with the program altogether, there were plenty of areas where Washington could draw back. The administration appeared to be sending this signal when, in July 1990, it postponed regular sessions of the Joint Political Military Group and the Joint Security Assistance Program group scheduled for September that were intended to deal, in part, with future US aid commitments. The reason given for the postponement was the delay in finishing budget deliberations in the United States. However the decision, taken shortly after the formation of the new Shamir government, also served to put off any US commitment on aid until after the new government had had a chance to demonstrate its approach to the peace process.

Meanwhile, the administration was finally beginning to make the hard decisions related to the reshaping of its defense posture. On the morning of the invasion of Kuwait, Secretary Cheney and JCS Chairman General Powell were scheduled to brief Congress on the reshaping of the US force posture; a major presidential speech was planned on the same subject. The tremendous changes that were certain to be announced would unquestionably affect Israel. The political context in which relevant decisions would be made thus seemed even more important.

But administration plans for dramatic drawdowns of units and equipment from Europe, worldwide force reductions, and force restructuring would all be pushed aside as planning began for what became the largest US military operation since World War II. Whatever consequences there might have been for Israel regarding either political or defense relations with the US were also put on hold. The new conflict would eventually raise more questions than it answered regarding the importance of US-Israeli strategic cooperation.

Chapter 7. Storm Clouds Over the Gulf

Difficult Choices and Decisions

Ostensibly, the war in the Gulf and US-Israeli strategic cooperation should not have interacted. The US had made clear since the early 1980s that it saw no role for Israel in the Gulf, and it would spend the better part of the conflict trying to ensure that Israel did indeed stay out. Ironically, it was at Saddam Hussein's insistence that Israel became involved. This, in turn, ushered in the most dramatic test of US-Israeli strategic cooperation in its eight-year history.

The Iraqi invasion of Kuwait on August 2, 1990 set in sharp relief the difficult choices confronting American policymakers regarding Israel. For 40-odd years they had been juggling competing interests related to the Arab world and the State of Israel. In the past, the dilemma had been to reconcile the hostility between the two camps in order to have good relations with both. If this policy had not worked at any given time, it constituted a setback for US diplomacy but did not directly put at risk American interests or lives.

In August 1990, however, the stakes of choosing the correct path between Israel and the Arabs became much higher: this time, the lives of hundreds of thousands of American troops were at risk. If the US alienated its potential Arab allies because of cooperation with Israel, it could find itself unable effectively to confront Saddam Hussein. On the other hand, neither did the US wish to eschew any valuable assistance that might make its job easier in the Gulf.

As Washington considered its options in the region, it weighed the considerable assets that had been built up in Saudi Arabia over the years, including US-built air bases, prepositioned stocks of Saudi equipment, a massive logistic infrastructure, and vital hardware such as the AWACS, needed for ensuring aerial superiority in the area. These assets — some of which seemed grossly in excess of Saudi needs when built — would be absolutely essential to any military effort against Iraq. Moreover, were they to be seized in an Iraqi move against Saudi Arabia, the loss of huge quantities of high-tech weaponry and hardware and modern facilities would have been devastating.

Further afield, there were potential Arab allies in Egypt as well as in the Gulf states of Bahrain, Oman and the UAE. While not on the front line, these states could provide staging opportunities or logistical support for coalition forces. Turkey, of course, was a NATO ally, had extensive experience in cooperating with and supporting US defense objectives, possessed substantial military power in its own right, and shared a long common border with Iraq.

And then there was Israel, the strongest single power in the region, which happened also to be a strategic ally of the United States. Israel had the most sophisticated, technically-advanced, and compatible facilities in the region as well as a formal program of strategic cooperation with the United States. While Israel remained an outcast in the region and represented the one issue that could possibly distract the Arab states' attention away from their unhappiness with Saddam Hussein, President Bush could count on Israel to share his intense concern over the Iraqi invasion and to support a strong American response.

Indeed, in the initial days following the US decision to deploy troops to Saudi Arabia, there was excited speculation in the Israeli press as to what Israel could do to assist the US. It was reported that Prime Minister Shamir had offered President Bush any help that America might need. Israeli defense officials, as well as Housing Minister Ariel Sharon and Science Minister Yuval Ne'eman were all quoted in the press as saying that Israel would respond positively to any US request for assistance. Initial commentaries contrasted Washington's renewed focus on security issues with the erosion of US-Israel relations that had occurred over the peace process, and predicted better days ahead for Israel as the US came to appreciate Israel's significance in confronting Saddam Hussein.[1]

But whether key officials in Washington ever seriously considered relying on Israel as a full partner against Saddam Hussein seems doubtful. Saudi Arabia was obviously the key to any massive deployment of troops to the area and its sensitivities regarding Israel were well known. If there was any doubt on this score, King Fahd reportedly made known his opposition to any involvement on the part of Israel during a phone conversation with President Bush the day of the invasion.[2]

There was also the question of coordination between Israel and CENTCOM, which would be running the American military campaign and which had earned a reputation for hostility toward Israel over the years. While by now Israel had developed very good military-to-military channels with the US, its regional interlocutory was the European Command (EUCOM). The mechanisms and personal relationships for cooperation between Israel and CENTCOM simply were not in place.

Thus the first phone call reportedly made by the US to any Middle Eastern state on the night Iraq invaded Kuwait went from Robert Kimmitt, under secretary of state for political affairs, to Israel's ambassador in Washington.[3] His message was that Washington wanted Israel to "keep its head down and its guns holstered."

This marked the beginning of the "low-profile" by Israel, so low in fact that President Bush avoided any personal contact with Prime Minister Shamir until December 1990.[4] Trips made throughout the region that fall by Secretary of State Baker and Secretary of Defense Cheney, as well as by President Bush, noticeably left Israel off their itineraries. From August 1990 to January 15, 1991, Secretary Baker conducted 10 missions abroad and held more than 200 meetings with various foreign representatives on the Gulf crisis — but less than a handful were with Israeli officials.[5] When it became clear that even Syria was being wooed as part of the allied coalition effort, the irony for Israel was complete.

Maintaining a low profile was obviously not an easy role for Israel to accept. The implicit labeling of Israel as a "liability" after so many years of acceptance as a contributor and partner to US interests in the region raised anew fears that the country was losing its strategic value. It was a short jump for some observers to conclude that the lack of a role in the Gulf crisis, coming so soon after the Soviet rationale had apparently been pulled out from under strategic cooperation, meant that Israel no longer had any value for the United States. On August 15, *Ha'aretz* commentator

Akiva Eldar wrote that, "The war in the Persian Gulf threatens to destroy the legend of Israel as a frontline base for the United States against half-crazy oil pirates."[6] A *Jerusalem Post* analysis pointed out that "the notion" of Israel as America's regional enforcer, or even as a staging ground for American intervention in the region, had collapsed.[7]

This theme was increasingly heard both inside Israel and beyond. An important Egyptian official stated in October that Israel's sideline role had "destroyed the credibility" of its claim to be a vital strategic ally of Washington.[8] Skepticism was also heard in the United States, particularly following the October 8 Temple Mount riot in which 17 Palestinians were killed. Syndicated columnists Evans and Novak published an article entitled, "Israel is no longer Washington's Partner." *Time Magazine* almost gleefully reported that the decision to cancel Egypt's debt marked the first time that Egypt would receive a better deal from the US than Israel.[9] This, *Time* declared, was "a stark reminder to Israelis of their diminishing importance as a strategic ally in the region."[10]

The problem with this line of analysis, of course, was that US policy had never envisioned a role for Israel in the Persian Gulf. This had applied even during the previous decade, when US contingency planning for the Gulf revolved around a possible Soviet threat, and despite the fact that the stated raison d'etre of US-Israeli strategic cooperation was a Soviet threat to the region. If maintaining Israel's distance from the Gulf had been considered so sensitive and important, then the sudden existence of a unique Arab versus Arab conflict there could only heighten Washington's concern that Israel not become involved. Thus, the ramifications of Israel's low profile for its strategic value should not have even been at issue. But due to the confusing legacy of strategic cooperation, this was neither well-known nor understood.

On the defensive to explain the low-profile policy, Israeli officials were quick to point out the irrelevancy of the Gulf for strategic cooperation. In an interview with *Ma'ariv* on August 6, 1990, Defense Minister Arens stated that the strategic cooperation agreement was "unrelated" to the events in the Gulf. Two days later, asked if he was disappointed that the US had not appealed to Israel for help, Arens responded in the negative, and noted that

Israel had understood since 1983 that the US did not wish it to be involved in the event that US forces were ever deployed to Saudi Arabia, or if Washington needed to enlist other forms of Arab cooperation.

This same point was echoed by Yosi Ben-Aharon, director general of the Prime Minister's Office, on August 14. Disputing reports that Israel's standing had diminished as a result of the developing coalition between the US and its Arab partners, Ben-Aharon stated that Israel had never constituted the United States' only bastion in the Middle East and that Israel "was not a major or even a secondary" player in the Gulf.[11] Foreign Minister Levy, asked a similar question, sharply responded that "people seemed to think that Israel was some sort of foreign legion base or expeditionary task force that was only waiting for someone to press a button." Levy had put his own finger exactly on the problem: that indeed was what many people thought about Israel's strategic importance for the United States.[12]

Testing the Alliance

The next five months between Iraq's invasion and the onset of hostilities would be marked by a dynamic of mounting tension between Washington's repeated insistence that Israel stay out of the conflict, and equally firm Israeli statements grudgingly accepting a low profile but also warning that, if the country were attacked, it would retaliate. At the heart of the problem were different assessments in Washington and Jerusalem over the threat facing Israel and the way it should be countered. This in turn generated intense disagreement as to the necessity of engaging in military coordination between the two sides.

From Israel's perspective, the low-profile requested by Washington was not an unreasonable demand. Israeli leaders recognized as well as anyone else that Israel's broader interests lay with the success of the anti-Iraq coalition, and that any overt Israeli role in the campaign against Saddam Hussein could queer the entire effort. This was politics, Middle East style.

But Israel also expected that, after having accepted the low-profile, quiet US-Israeli cooperation would take place on those aspects of the crisis that threatened directly to affect Israel, such as an Iraqi missile attack on Israel or an Iraqi military move into Jordan. Specifically, Israel wanted real-time intelligence that would allow it to know immediately if Saddam Hussein was preparing to fire missiles at Israel; a communications network that would facilitate emergency coordination of Israeli activity with US forces; and tactical coordination between the two countries' air forces which would allow Israel to retaliate against targets in Iraq without running the risk of conflict with American air force units operating in the same region.

In other words, Israel believed that if war broke out, it was likely to be attacked. And if Israel were attacked, it would respond. There was even a perception on the part of many Israeli experts that, once the war broke out, the US would see Israel's strength as an asset to be used in the military campaign against Iraq.[13] Thus the low-profile was hardly a permanent condition, but rather a tactical ploy that made sense all around.

Gradually, however, it became clear that Washington viewed Israel's sideline role not as a temporary phenomenon but as an essential condition for the success of its Gulf policies. Indeed, as Israel settled into its low-profile and US efforts to build an anti-Iraq coalition bore fruit, a positive linkage was established between the two which further maintained the notion that Israel must be kept as far away from the Gulf as possible. This was fed by Saddam Hussein's efforts early on to split the coalition by charging the US and Israel with secret collusion (e.g., he claimed that painted-over Israeli aircraft were operating out of Saudi airbases).

There was also a certain ambivalence in Washington's thinking regarding the likelihood that Israel would be drawn into the conflict. While US planners could not ignore Iraq's repeated threats to attack Israel, from a rational military perspective such an attack simply did not make sense, given the limited damage that Iraq could inflict on Israel and the seemingly certain retaliation that it would bring down on itself. Particularly as the initial days passed following the invasion and nothing happened vis-a-vis Israel, there was a tendency to place the problem of an attack on Israel behind the more pressing concerns of deploying thousands of US troops overseas and building an international coalition.

The net result was that, as Israel pressed for coordination that would allow it to retaliate in the event of an attack, Washington saw its demands as unrealistic. As one senior US official was quoted as saying, Israel wanted "a level of coordination that is more than is required."[14] Or, as *Ha'aretz* military analyst Zeev Schiff was told by Pentagon officials, at a time when Washington was going to such pains to set up an Arab coalition against another Arab country, it was not appropriate to "get preoccupied with Israel on hypothetical war scenarios."[15]

Adding to Washington's reticence was an obvious reluctance to give Israel the means that would allow it to act independently against Iraq. There was a fear that real-time intelligence could give Israel the information needed to preempt an Iraqi attack, which Washington wanted to avoid at all costs. By the same token, providing Israel with the IFF (Identification Friend or Foe) codes needed to ensure that US and Israeli aircraft did not enter into combat with one another, was likely to be interpreted as a "green light" by Israel, allowing it to retaliate against Iraq at will. Both suggestions were directly at odds with Washington's efforts to keep Israeli actions under some form of US control.

Thus until late in the crisis Washington refused to engage in any operational coordination with Israel or even to discuss scenarios that involved Israel being drawn into the conflict. While Israel wanted to discuss the details of each country's response, the US did not want to discuss any Israeli response at all.

The one area where Washington did feel comfortable engaging in close cooperation was in the realm of intelligence and information exchange. While the US turned down Israel's request for an independent link to US satellite information, it appears to have made every effort to share available intelligence on Iraq with Israel and vice versa. Indeed, this cooperation was reportedly so extensive that the US apparently was sending some of its photo intelligence to Israel for closer examination and assessment by Israeli experts. This obviously was not simply a hand-holding exercise for Israel but a program considered to have real benefit for the United States.

Bribes and Promises

The US recognized, however, that keeping Israel on the sidelines would involve more than a policy of denial. At any time Israel could play a spoiler role if it perceived that its security interests were being threatened. It thus behooved Washington to try to reassure Israel that its interests were being looked after, and to instill confidence on the part of Israeli leaders as to American determination to remove the Iraqi threat to the region.

This strategic interest in reassuring Israel was buttressed by domestic political realities, which demanded a solid show of support for Israel. On the eve of the Iraqi invasion, the entire question of future aid levels to Israel had been up in the air. Israel had assurances that aid levels would be maintained through FY1991, but had received no such promise for FY1992. Now, with the threat of an attack on Israel, and in the wake of proposed new arms sales to Saudi Arabia and the US decision to forgive Egypt's debt, political pressures grew for increased military assistance to Israel.

Following visits to Washington by both Defense Minister Arens and Foreign Minister Levy in September 1990, Secretary Baker announced agreement on supplemental aid. To improve Israel's defenses, two Patriot missile units, valued at about $114 million, would be provided as grant aid; to reinforce Israel's deterrent capability 15 F-15 aircraft and 10 CH-53 helicopters were promised; finally, the delivery of $100 million worth of munitions for prepositioning in Israel already approved by Congress would be accelerated.[16] No promises were made, however, for an increase in Israel's annual security assistance of $1.8 billion (Arens had reportedly been seeking $2.5 billion).

Israel's supporters in Congress took the issue even further, pushing through additional aid for FY1991 that, if implemented, was potentially worth more than $1 billion.[17] The most important element of this was drawdown authority for $700 million worth of US military stocks in Europe to be transferred to Israel. These comprised a variety of weapons systems, including defensive radar, helicopters and modern combat aircraft (some, such as the F-15, already promised by the administration, as noted above).

Congress also called for the prepositioning of $200 million of American equipment in Israel, the stockpiling there of 4.5 million barrels of fuel worth some $485 million, and the identification of funds for dredging the Port of Haifa so that US aircraft carriers could dock there. This legislation underscored once again the power of the congressional purse in deciding one of the fundamental parameters of the US-Israeli relationship.

The second aspect of administration efforts to convince Israel to stay on the sidelines concerned contingencies for American action in the event of an attack on Israel. In the early days of the conflict, as Washington sought to keep its response to Iraq's invasion completely separate from any possible Israeli linkage, its commitment to Israel in the face of Iraqi threats was decidedly vague. Asked by reporters in late August if the US would help defend Israel against an Iraqi chemical attack, President Bush commented that Israel "never had any difficulty defending itself."[18] This same theme of Israel's ability to defend itself — thereby alleviating the US of the necessity to draw it into defense plans — had also been struck by US Representative Robert Michel and US Senator Robert Dole shortly after the invasion occurred.[19]

But in the face of continuing vitriolic threats against Israel by Saddam Hussein, administration comments regarding the US commitment to Israel's security were beefed up. This was probably intended not only as a signal and deterrent to Baghdad but also to reassure an Israeli government that, if insecure, would be more likely to strike out. Thus, during a meeting with Foreign Minister Levy in late September, Secretary Baker emphasized the United States' absolute commitment to Israel's security and told Levy that he could "count on that fact" if Israel was attacked by Iraq.[20] But Baker apparently stopped short of stating categorically that the US would be prepared to commit American forces to Israel's defense in the event of attack; he also proved reluctant to repeat his comments publicly.[21]

Meanwhile, events in Israel would leave the administration in even more of a quandary regarding its posture. Following the Temple Mount incident of October 8, the US voted in the UN Security Council to condemn Israel — the first time it had censured Jerusalem since the 1982 invasion of Lebanon. The administration also applied heavy pressure on the Israeli government to cooperate with a proposed UN investigation team looking into the event.

But despite the real and serious differences between the Bush Administration and the Shamir government over the Palestinian issue, it was not in the United States' interest to foster the impression of a rift between the two governments at such a sensitive time. Thus, the administration tried to mute its public criticism of Israel while at the same time reaffirming the "unshakable" US commitment to its security. Time and again Secretary Baker reiterated this commitment in testimony on Capitol Hill, even opining that Israel's security was enhanced by the presence of American troops in Saudi Arabia.[22]

Yet Israel's defense never became an important part of Washington's public posture on the Gulf buildup. The only clear, explicit statement of US military support for Israel came in little-noticed testimony to the House Foreign Affairs Committee by Assistant Secretary John Kelly in mid-September, when he noted that "Saddam should be under no misapprehensions that any move against Israel would be immediately retaliated against by the US."[23] This statement was never picked up by the major newspapers in the United States; moreover, less than two weeks later, Baker declined to repeat it publicly.[24]

Another example of Israel's sporadic role in American security policy statements came when Defense Secretary Cheney announced the deployment of at least 100,000 more US troops to the Gulf in late October. To one reporter — Wolf Blitzer, who was a well-known journalist in Israel before signing up with CNN — Cheney justified the increase by saying that the US had to be ready for the possibility that Saddam "might lash out at Israel, might lash out at the Saudi oil fields."[25] But Cheney spoke on three other TV programs that day about the troop increase, and in none of them was Israel mentioned.[26]

Thus, from the US perspective, the public record on defending Israel was, at best, low-key and not completely clear.[27] As for Israeli leaders, they wanted not a US pledge to come to Israel's aid, but rather operational coordination that would allow Israel full freedom of action in the event of an attack from Iraq. As Prime

Minister Shamir noted in early December, "We have always told the US that Israel is capable of defending itself. We only asked the US to supply us with the means to do so and with the requisite conditions."[28]

By mid-November, Israel was reportedly increasingly considering whether it should go it alone.[29] For Israelis this was hardly an academic issue. If the US had a trump card to play in the form of denying Israel the electronic codes needed to avoid conflict with US forces in the area, Israel also had a trump card — albeit a risky one — of independent action. Sensitive to the pressure that had been exerted by the US in the past not to act, particularly before the 1973 war (restraint that had contributed to a significant loss of lives in the initial days of fighting), Israeli leaders had their own set of security-related calculations, that were not necessarily identical to those of the United States. As Zeev Schiff had warned the previous month, "Even if we want to coordinate moves with our friends, we may well be forced to go it alone. Whoever wants to reduce that possibility must foster a certain coordination with Israel."[30]

But from Washington's perspective, even if one believed that Israeli retaliation was inevitable (as some officials clearly did), administration officials were reluctant to give Israel a priori approval for the operations it appeared to be insisting on. Thus, both sides seemed to approach the problem from an all-or-nothing perspective: military planners on both sides were willing neither to reveal their plans in full nor to give up control over any aspect of the conflict. As Schiff commented, "neither side wants to reveal its operational plans in advance or limit its freedom of action. We don't expect the Americans to tell us what they will do, and we don't want them to ask us what we will do."[31] It was this attitude of fierce independence on both sides that lay at the heart of the problem.

On November 7, the Joint Political Military Group and the Joint Security Assistance Planning Group gathered for their previously-delayed annual meeting to discuss strategic cooperation between the two countries. This was the only meeting of these coordinating bodies during the crisis and war. On the eve of the meeting, Defense Minister Arens sent a clear message about Israeli intentions to retaliate in the event of an attack, stating that "if Israel is attacked, its reaction will not be on a low profile" and noting that the IDF was prepared for any possibility.[32] But the meeting came and went without any resolution of the problem. One senior Israeli military officer expressed doubt that, in the event of war, Washington even had plans to go after the Iraqi missiles as a matter of first priority.[33] Meanwhile, some Israeli military officers hinted that Washington's refusal to coordinate with Israel might lead Israel to launch a preemptive strike against Iraq. While this neither accorded with official Israeli statements, which held that Israel would not preempt, nor reflected a consensus within Israel, it did serve to underscore the level of frustration building within Israel.

A Turning Point

The turning point in this stand-off came in December. As the US increasingly prepared for war, Iraqi threats that Israel would be attacked in the event of war became even more explicit. As if to buttress these claims, Iraq test-fired two missiles in early December, for the first time since April. The Iraqi missile launchings not only underscored the genuineness of the Iraqi threat but, even more important, they highlighted the inadequacy of coordination between the US and Israel to deal with such an attack. Israeli sources reported that US surveillance detected the launch only after the missile had been in the air for several minutes, and then failed to warn Israel that a warhead was "headed" in its direction.[33] As the US was forced to consider how to deal with this situation, it became clear that more assets would have to be devoted to the problem, and better means of communication established with Israel.

Meanwhile, even though President Bush was by now firmly on a course leading to war with Iraq, publicly this was not so clear. In early December Bush announced his willingness to open a dialogue with Saddam Hussein before the January 15 deadline expired. This raised additional concerns in Israel that the US might be tempted to cut a deal with Saddam at Israel's expense, both in terms of the Palestinian issue and with regard to Iraq's military power. Given the increasingly high stakes of the looming conflict, any such miscommunications or misunderstandings between the US and Israel potentially put at risk the administration's overall policy in the Gulf. Thus, after much speculation as to whether the president would receive Prime Minister Shamir during the latter's visit to the States in December, the White House finally announced on November 28 that the meeting would indeed be held.

Thus on December 11 Prime Minister Shamir was received by President Bush at the White House, the first time the two men had spoken since the conflict had begun. Shamir undoubtedly was briefed on the president's overall plans for war, and received assurances that there was no interest in cutting a last-minute deal with Saddam Hussein that would leave either his prestige or military power intact. Shamir, for his part, expressed full support for the president and his policies. Thus, notwithstanding the differences between the two men, they possessed a common view of the threat that Saddam Hussein posed to their countries and were united in their determination to do what was necessary to eradicate that threat.

Specifically, President Bush received a promise from Shamir that not only would there be no preemptive Israeli strike on Iraq, but that before Israel responded to an attack by Iraq, Shamir would "consult" with the US. In return for this promise of prior consultations, Bush finally agreed to measures that would allow at least some operational coordination between the two sides in the event of war. This took the form of a secure, dedicated communications link between the Pentagon and the Israel Defense Ministry in Tel Aviv, code-named Hammer Rick.[35] The link provided three benefits for Israel: first, it established a secure "hotline" between the two countries that allowed minute-by-minute coordination by the two defense ministers if need be; secondly, it established a direct means for the passing of early, real-time warnings to Israel of Scud launches detected by US satellites; and finally, it created a de facto means of communication between Israel and US command authorities in Saudi Arabia, via Washington, that underscored Israel's special relationship to the allied coalition.

The one asset that the US was still not willing to grant was access to the IFF codes that Israel would need in order actually to carry out an operation against Iraq without running the risk of engaging in conflict with US forces. Thus, despite the closer coordination between the two sides, and notwithstanding Shamir's promise to first "consult" before launching any counter-strike, the US chose to retain for itself that final element of control over the situation. It was a US operation, after all, involving hundreds of thousands of American lives. With so much at stake, even a longtime friend could perhaps not be entirely trusted.

Instead of giving Israel the ability to act itself, the US committed itself to acting on Israel's behalf. During their meeting, President Bush assured Shamir as to the US commitment to respond in the event of an Iraqi attack on Israel, and he briefed Shamir on concrete plans that the US had developed to destroy fixed Iraqi Scud launcher sites in western Iraq, as well as mobile launchers in the area.[36] By opening such a dialogue, the president created an opportunity for Israel to comment on the plans and to suggest, based on its own extensive planning for dealing with the threat, possible modifications or improvements.

While this was not exactly what Israel had been seeking, it went a long way toward enhancing Jerusalem's confidence regarding the missile threat itself. Real-time warning was vital in order to ensure that the Israeli population had time to prepare for an attack. The US commitment to act in the event of an Iraqi strike on Israel meant that Israel was not facing an enemy alone (although the long-term ramifications of Israel's consequent restraint for the credibility of Israel's deterrent — particularly in view of Israel's by now frequent threats to retaliate — would remain an issue of acute concern for Israel). And Washington's willingness to share with Israel its concrete plans for destroying the Iraqi missile threat at least gave Israeli military planners a back door for helping to ensure Israel's security. The basis was thus laid for more significant cooperation.

Chapter 8. Israel Under Attack

On the Eve of War

While the Bush-Shamir discussions in December 1990 constituted a significant breakthrough in relations between the two countries, the proof of closer coordination would only come through the translation of the new commitments into practical policies. Even as the complex task was turned over to the respective bureaucracies, Washington was already preoccupied with the job of preparing for a war ultimately involving over 400,000 of its own troops.

The result was that, as the deadline for war quickly approached, the "hardware" part of the delicate equation worked out between the two leaders was lagging considerably behind the dialogue. The drawdown of $700 million worth of American weapons and their transfer to Israel was being held up, as US commanders in the Gulf considered their own needs and as US commanders in Europe were already being taxed by the tremendous demands of transferring stocks to the Gulf. Neither the F-15 aircraft or the CH-53 helicopters promised to Israel by Secretary Baker had arrived.

And, in a development that would have the most direct consequences for the war, the Patriot missile system was not operational before the start of hostilities. Some of the elements of the two Patriot batteries promised by the US the previous fall arrived in Israel on January 11. But the Israeli crews selected to man the system were still undergoing training in Texas and were not scheduled to return to Israel until the end of January. Meanwhile, there were reports that the Patriot missiles themselves as well as the software needed to operate the system would not arrive until April.[1]

While there would be much subsequent finger-pointing as to who was to blame for the delay, the fact that only two Patriot batteries were planned at all suggests that neither side was seized with the problem of providing an active defense for Israel. The US was preoccupied with other events and, in any event, felt that it could not afford to give any more systems to Israel without cutting into defense requirements for its own troops in the Gulf. For

Israel's part, military planners had always viewed with great ambivalence the prospect of using scarce resources on a system considered inadequate for Israel's defense needs. From their perspective, the way to deal with the Iraqi missile threat was the traditional use of air power and other offensive capabilities to take out the Iraqi launchers. Over the longer term, Israelis were counting on their own highly-sophisticated Arrow ATBM system, which was still under development.

As it happened, the only effective means for countering Iraqi Scud missiles as war approached was indeed offensive action directed at destroying the launchers. While Jerusalem did not appear too uncomfortable with this state of affairs, believing in the IDF's ability to thwart any attack, Washington clearly saw the situation as potentially disastrous, since it meant that Israel could very well be pulled into the war due to the lack of any reasonable alternatives to defend itself.

Thus, with only four days to go before the UN-imposed deadline for the withdrawal of Iraqi forces from Kuwait, the president hurriedly sent a personal envoy, Deputy Secretary of State Lawrence Eagleburger, to Israel for a last-minute effort to coordinate US and Israeli policies. Eagleburger had been one of the instrumental players behind strategic cooperation in 1983. Considered in Jerusalem to be one of those rare friends who was driven not by ideological sympathy with Israel but by realpolitik concerns of the United States, Eagleburger was the perfect candidate to establish a more practical working relationship that would meet the needs of both sides. He was accompanied by Defense Under Secretary Paul Wolfowitz, also considered a long-time friend of Israel's.

The visit apparently resulted in two rather important disagreements.[2] First, Eagleburger offered Israel immediate delivery of two of the most advanced Patriot missile batteries, with American crews to operate them. This offer was turned down by the Israeli leadership, who preferred to take the risk of having no active defenses rather than setting the disturbing precedent of allowing American soldiers to defend Israeli territory. Moreover, from their perspective, the offer was too little and came too late; with the war just a few days off, Israel was apparently banking on air power (both American and Israeli) to destroy the Iraqi threat before it inflicted serious damage on Israeli soil.[3]

Secondly, Eagleburger requested that Israel refrain from military action in the Gulf even if Israel were attacked by Iraq, a request which was repeated publicly in Washington by National Security Adviser Brent Scowcroft. This too was firmly but politely rebuffed by Israeli leaders, who saw the defense of Israel as a job that could not be transferred to another country, no matter how friendly. As Shamir noted to the Israeli Cabinet, it was the government's prerogative to decide how Israel would respond in the event of an Iraqi attack. And, as he emphasized to Eagleburger, under no circumstances could Israel give up its sovereign right to self-defense by pledging not to retaliate if attacked.[4] Defense Minister Arens reemphasized this following his talks with Eagleburger: "If attacked we will respond."[5]

But despite these important public differences, the two days of intense consultations marked a turning point with regard to genuine US and Israeli coordination of policies. In the course of discussions, Prime Minister Shamir made clear that he stood by his commitment to President Bush in December to "consult" before taking any action. While he could not make any a priori commitments, Shamir articulated the three factors that would go into any Israeli response: the extent of damage from attack, the perceived effect on Israel's long-term deterrent posture, and, perhaps most important, the degree to which the US Air Force was successful in removing the threat of repeated missile attacks on Israel.[6]

This private explanation of Israel's retaliation policy appears to have gone a long way toward dispelling distrust in Washington that Israel was intent on retaliation at all costs. Shamir clearly drew a distinction between the tough public message that was intended for Saddam Hussein, and a nuanced private position which was based on very real and rational strategic considerations. This candid exchange of views would not only help to build confidence between the two sides, it also led to a significant, albeit belated, change in Washington's own public posture. Recognizing that its public demands on Israel not to retaliate had been a mistake — since they only served to diminish overall deterrence against Iraq — administration officials upon Eagleburger's return quickly moved to a line that underscored Israel's right to exercise self-defense and to make its own defense-related decisions.[7]

Meanwhile, with the clock running out, Eagleburger did make some progress on operational coordination between the two sides. While many details were left unresolved (e.g., the US still would not agree to give Israel the IFF codes needed to allow it to act securely in the same theater of operations as US forces in the Gulf), the US did agree upon Eagleburger's return to Washington to establish a "joint coordinating apparatus," according to Israeli Foreign Minister Levy.[8] This was probably a reference to the Hammer Rick communications link between the IDF and the Pentagon that became operational on Sunday, January 13.[9]

The two sides also reached an understanding regarding the US commitment to go after the Scud launchers aimed at Israel from the very start of the war.[10] President Bush promised that Cheney would give the Israelis advance notice before any offensive operation was commenced.[11] In the event, Cheney used the Hammer Rick line two hours before the first attack on Iraqi forces to inform Israeli Defense Minister Arens that the offensive was being launched.[12]

Thus, the overall effect of Eagleburger's visit was to mark a decided change in Washington's "hands-off" approach to coordination with Israel. Notably, Eagleburger was not merely the first high-level emissary to visit Israel since the outbreak of the war, his was the highest-level US diplomatic mission to Israel since President Bush had taken office in January 1989. While a wholesale change did not occur overnight, the visit helped to reinstitute a genuine dialogue between the leaders of both countries which, in turn, contributed to a new sense of trust and confidence between them.

Without a doubt, this had an important effect on the way Israeli leaders viewed the situation. Indeed, the last statement made by Prime Minister Shamir before Israel was attacked, expressed his confidence that Israel was "stronger than ever." Testifying to the importance of the Eagleburger mission, Shamir stated that Israel was not committed to an automatic retaliation but reserved the right to decide for itself whether and how it would respond.[13]

Desert Storm Crashes into Israel

Following the expiration of the January 15 UN deadline for Iraqi withdrawal from Kuwait, the US launched a massive aerial offensive against Iraq. For one day, Israel held its breath, hoping that the early reports of dramatic Allied successes against Iraqi targets, including the Iraqi missile launchers that the US had pledged to destroy, meant that Israel was spared from attack.

This hope was quickly dispelled in the early morning hours of January 18, when Israel came under missile attack from Iraq. Eight missiles hit the Tel Aviv area; one landed in Haifa. Amazingly, no direct deaths resulted from the attack. But as Israel awakened to the shattering reality of vulnerability in the missile age, the days ahead seemed very bleak indeed. There was not only a dreaded expectation of further missile attacks, there was also a palpable fear that the next attack would entail the use of chemical warheads.

As far as Israel's population was concerned, that first night of attack, which was followed the day after by another salvo of ten missiles, many of which landed in Tel Aviv, did not say much about the efficacy of US-Israeli coordination. Confidence in the military's ace in the hole — that the launchers would be destroyed by massive American bombardment — was shattered. Meanwhile, despite more than a year of US-Israeli discussions about Patriot missiles, Israel had absolutely no means with which to fend off the Scuds. Finally, compared with early Israeli expectations that there might be a couple of hours of warning time before an attack, in reality many Israelis heard missiles landing before they heard any warning at all.

Thus, the key issue for both Israeli and American leaders immediately following the attack was how best to protect Israel. Thwarting further attacks and, failing that, diminishing the effects of missile attacks were obviously the key issues. But these could not be divorced from two other, more general considerations: ensuring the overall success of the US-led allied campaign against Iraq, and preserving Israel's future deterrent posture in the region.

While there would be some disagreement over the tactics to

achieve these objectives, the two countries would discover, somewhat to their surprise, that there was no disagreement over the objectives themselves. Coming after a period when some American officials seemed to believe that Israel simply wanted to complicate US-Arab relations, and some Israeli officials believed that the new administration simply did not care about Israel, the recognition of mutual interests further contributed to the new basis of trust and understanding that had begun during the Eagleburger visit before the war. This broad understanding was absolutely essential to US and Israeli efforts to establish coordination and cooperation under wartime conditions.

Minutes after the Iraqi attack on Israel, Secretary Baker called Arens who, after talking with Prime Minister Shamir, subsequently called Cheney on the newly-established Hammer Rick hotline.[14] Obviously concerned to prevent further attacks, Arens insisted on an immediate upgrade of military coordination so that Israel could act against the Iraqi missile launchers. Specifically, Arens sought a slot during which US operations would steer well clear of the areas Israel sought to attack, as well as a cleared air corridor through Saudi Arabia or Jordan.

This was exactly what the administration feared would lead to a possible widening of the war and the fracturing of the anti-Iraq coalition. According to sources interviewed after the war, Israel's plans called for an Israeli armed sweep through western Iraq by helicopter gunships and ground forces, including commando teams, all protected by Israel Air Force planes that traversed a secured air corridor through Jordan or Saudi Arabia.[15] Given Jordan's vow to resist any Israeli overflight of its territory, implementation of such an Israeli plan could have led to a full-scale war between Israel and Jordan, which in turn might have brought Syria in on the side of Jordan. The net effect, from Washington's perspective, would have been serious and possibly disastrous for the campaign against Saddam Hussein.

Thus, during a second telephone conversation with Shamir later that day, President Bush presented a package of measures to Shamir aimed at convincing Israel that it was not necessary for it to take military action.[16] First, Bush promised an even more intensive US effort against the Scud launchers and even closer coordination and information-sharing with Israel regarding the US campaign.[17] Also, an American major general from JCS Chairman Powell's personal staff was assigned to Israel for as long as necessary to serve as an indirect liaison between the Israeli military and CENTCOM. And, perhaps of greatest importance for the Israeli population, the president ordered the airlift of four Patriot batteries to Israel, together with their American crews.

One other decision by President Bush with far-reaching consequences was to send Deputy Secretary Eagleburger (and Defense Under Secretary Paul Wolfowitz) back to Israel; Bush told Shamir that he should "talk to him (Eagleburger) as if you are talking to me." Eagleburger's presence on the ground during the next week would be absolutely vital as Israel worked its way through its restraint policy in the face of repeated missile attacks. His role would be less to hold Israel back than to engage in genuine dialogue with Israeli leaders at a time when US and Israeli interests had been inextricably linked. His decision to spend several nights at a downtown Tel Aviv hotel dramatized the administration's determination not to abandon Israel under attack.

While all of these moves were welcomed in Israel, still the key factor affecting any decision to retaliate was the question whether there was some unique role that Israel could play which would make a difference in its situation. From the US perspective, there was nothing that the Israel Air Force could do that the US was not already doing or was willing to do. The Israel Air Force was less certain. Air Force Commander Avihu Bin Nun reportedly expressed confidence during a Defense Cabinet meeting that the missile launcher problem could be taken care of as soon as the political leadership gave the word. On the eve of war, Bin Nun argued that it was not easy to destroy the missile bases but that Israel "had developed in the last several months tactics and techniques" for attacking the sites and "has the capacity of doing it if necessary."[18] There also was considerable concern that by not acting, Israel's deterrent posture vis-a-vis the Arab countries would be gravely weakened.

These arguments by themselves, however, were not persuasive in the face of US determination to thwart the missile threat. If the

Israel Air Force was simply planning to do what the US was doing but perhaps better, Israel's leadership had good reason to look closely at the risks. And, indeed, the risks of carrying out a retaliatory strike were potentially tremendous, both concerning the possible reaction from the neighboring countries of Syria and Jordan, and with regard to Israel's deterrent posture should such a strike fail in achieving its objectives. Throughout, there remained the real question about how a retaliatory strike could be coordinated with US forces in the face of continued American refusal to give Israel IFF codes.

Meanwhile, on the positive side of the ledger was the goodwill that Israel was chalking up by not acting, not only with the US but around the world. Also, Israel was lucky that the missiles had resulted in relatively few serious casualties. Perhaps the most compelling reason for restraint was offered by the prime minister at the end of a Defense Cabinet meeting two days after the initiation of attacks. Shamir reportedly summed up the situation by stating that, for Israel's long-term security, the most important thing was the destruction of Iraq's military capabilities. The Americans could do that. Nothing should be done to get in their way.[19] The rest of the leadership apparently agreed with him. The decision to defer, albeit not rule out, Israeli military action was reportedly unanimous.

A New Partnership

It thus was not simply Israel's policy of restraint that ushered in a new closeness in relations, but the underlying perception of mutual interests between the two countries upon which restraint rested. Both Shamir and Bush understood the game evidently being played by Saddam Hussein of trying to bring Israel into the conflict. The effort to foil this ploy created a de facto partnership in the Gulf War.

One essential element of this was the dialogue established at the highest-levels between the two countries. In sharp contrast to the prewar period, Shamir and Bush talked repeatedly during the course of the war, and Bush highlighted the US-Israeli relationship by publicly pledging support for Israel. Moreover, there was a greater sense of respect marking their relationship. The president emphasized again and again Israel's unquestionable right to respond, and scrupulously avoided any statement that might have suggested less than an equal partnership. Eagleburger underscored this during his stay in Israel, stressing that the relationship was very close, respectful and equal between the two countries. Shamir, for his part, repeatedly expressed his admiration for the US effort and the determination exhibited by the Gulf campaign.

A second element of the new partnership was a unique one for the relationship: the provision of the US Patriot systems with their American crews. The Patriot batteries were airlifted to Israel during the first weekend of the war in the largest delivery of US military hardware to Israel since the Yom Kippur War. IDF officials termed the operation, which involved 30 huge C-5 cargo planes, truly brilliant.[20] President Bush promised to double the number of batteries on January 23, following the most devastating Scud attack on Israel of the war.

Meanwhile, in a decision termed "extraordinary" in the January 19 Pentagon briefing, hundreds of US troops were stationed in Israel to man the Patriot batteries. The first American soldiers ever involved in military action in defense of Israel, the Patriot crews created a strong emotional and political bond between the two countries during the time they were there. (The deployment of American forces on Israeli soil also struck a discordant note among Israelis who were concerned at the precedent of dependence, albeit brief and limited, on foreign forces defending them.) On a more practical level, host country support and the development of an infrastructure system for the troops led to enhanced military-to-military cooperation.

Finally, less visible but crucial to the continuing viability of the restraint policy, was the increase in cooperation between the two sides related to the war itself. Ironically, the effort to keep Israel out of the war appears to have led to the blossoming of working-level operational coordination. While General Schwarzkopf commented after the war that "Israel didn't know everything we were doing,"[21] it was clear that the communications links and the assignment of a senior US Army officer in Israel, had contributed to significantly enhanced coordination.

The thrust of these efforts appears to have been aimed at involving Israel in US decisions and actions pertaining to search and destroy missions against the Iraqi missile launchers. In a briefing for the Knesset Foreign Affairs and Defense Committee at the end of January, Prime Minister Shamir stated that "The basis of our approach is agreement on mutual consultation concerning all moves taken in the sector from which the Scud missiles are launched."[22] His use of the word "mutual" clearly indicated that consultations were not simply a nod to Israel, but actually involved two-way discussions on how best to go after the missile threat in western Iraq. Cheney reaffirmed this after the war when he gave the name of the US general sent to Israel — Major General Mack Armstrong — and said that he had worked with the Israel Defense Forces in Tel Aviv "to give us better ideas about how we could go after the Scuds."[23]

Shamir went on to say that these consultations included exchanges of intelligence, discussion of operational ideas, and "coordination of measures" not further defined. He also referred to the special high-speed communications links (the Hammer Rick hotline) operating between the US and Israel, which underscored US and Israeli coordination in one of the most sensitive areas of American defense policy. Within seconds of detecting a Scud being launched from Iraq, an intricate series of steps were taken involving US defense satellites and ground-based systems, that eventually resulted in first a 90-second, and later a five-minute warning to Israel's civilian population.[24]

Shamir also stated during his briefing that contacts had been established to study "the forms and the parameters whereby such self-defense could be carried out, without impairing the success of the Gulf campaign as a whole." This suggests that, after months of Israeli requests, the US had finally agreed to at least hold discussions on specific scenarios under which Israel might retaliate.

But this was clearly one significant area of cooperation that did not bear much fruit. The best that appears to have come out of these discussions might be termed "no-coordination coordination." Throughout the course of the war, the US refused to coordinate with Israel on any planning for an Israeli retaliatory strike against the missile fields; nor did it release the IFF codes that would have allowed both air forces to operate in the same theater.

While this probably represents the closest either side came to finding a solution that met the minimal requirements of both, it was undoubtedly considered an unsatisfactory arrangement by military planners all around, and would continue to cause friction between the two sides until the close of the war. The Americans apparently did not want to provide the one missing piece that might open the door to an independent Israeli decision to retaliate, despite the fact that at an early stage the major Arab coalition partners actually stated their support for Israel's right to retaliate. Why did Washington remain so sensitive to this issue? Certainly the administration had an interest in avoiding anything that held out the least likelihood of undermining the coalition war effort. It is also possible that the US had promised the Arab states that there would be no actual coordination between US forces operating in the Gulf and Israeli forces.

For the Israelis, it was a question of pride, of their sovereign rights, and of the US imposing limits that were inconsistent with the strategic partnership. Israel Air Force Commander Bin Nun perhaps put it best when, in an extensive interview given in early February, he discussed the various forms of coordination between the US and Israel in the event of an Israeli action. The best coordination, he said, "is that of allies, in which they adapt themselves to each other and also give each other mutual help. That would be the highest level of coordination, the level I of course would want if we decide to act." But he also referred to a different type of coordination, "in which they evacuate the area as far as a certain line and we work freely there." While he acknowledged that this was also a way in which Israel could act to get the job done, it clearly was not the type of coordination expected between two allies against a common foe.[25]

Indeed, whether one viewed the cooperation that evolved during the war as a genuine example of partnership or as testimony to Israel's continued ambiguous strategic role, would depend on the original expectations that one held for US-Israeli cooperation. Certainly the war demonstrated the limits to that relationship in the face of sensitivities in the Arab world as perceived by US planners. Yet for those actually involved in the quiet cooperation that evolved between the two sides, the war vividly demonstrated not only the many ways that cooperation could benefit both sides, but also the maturity of a relationship that allowed cooperation to blossom under very difficult conditions.

What Legacy for Strategic Cooperation?

The full legacy of the war for strategic cooperation may not be felt for some time to come. Unlike earlier wars, such as in 1967 or 1973, which proved to be watersheds in many respects for US-Israeli strategic relations, the Gulf War appears to have strengthened already existing trends in the relationship rather than creating significant new ones. Where innovations did take place — e.g., the stationing of US forces in Israel, Israeli restraint in deference to American needs, cooperation with CENTCOM — these will likely be seen as exceptions to the rule, rather than the delineation of new norms in the relationship.

From the perspective of US strategic planners, the war could be seen as underscoring what they had long believed: Israel is too far away from the Gulf to be considered an essential or key player in a conflict there. Moreover, because of seemingly intractable differences between Israel and its Arab neighbors, even marginal involvement by Israel could have queered the entire US effort. All in all, the Gulf War proved that the US could conduct a major land war in the region, involving hundreds of thousands of troops, without any direct assistance from the strongest power in the region — Israel. As Egyptians in particular were quick to point out, Israel was no longer the sole strategic ally of the US in the region.

But that, of course, does not tell the entire story of Israel's role in the Gulf War. First, Israel had a technological contribution to make to the Allied war effort that testified to the efficacy of defense R&D cooperation through the years. A number of Israeli-produced systems were used effectively in the war by the US, including the Popeye air-to-surface missile and the Pioneer unmanned aerial vehicle deployed by both the US Navy and the Marine Corps for reconnaissance, surveillance and target-spotting missions, and for damage assessment. Another Israeli innovation, the Track Width Mine Plow, helped to breach Iraqi minefields.[26]

Secondly, Israel made a contribution in the area of intelligence and information exchange, both in the run-up to the Gulf War and during the war itself. This came to include a US-Israeli dialogue on tactics and methods to fight Iraq's missile capabilities in western Iraq, which produced some suggestions that were acted upon by Allied forces. Indeed, by the end of the war, the artificial divisions separating CENTCOM (long considered implacably hostile to any Israeli involvement) from EUCOM (of which Israel as well as Syria, Lebanon and Turkey were geographically a part) were all but erased, if only temporarily.

Third, Israel's relative importance vis-a-vis the Gulf has always been a function of how accessible and cooperative Arab states have been to American overtures. While the immediate impact of the Gulf War was the establishment of a powerful link between the US and the Arab world, US efforts following the war to codify this relationship have thus far met with less success. Should the United States be unable to convince enough governments to store weaponry and equipment in the region to speed future troop deployments, or to participate in joint exercises or provide facilities, Israel's relative stock vis-a-vis the Gulf might well go up.

Finally, as was noted earlier, the US had never attached to Israel strategic importance in relation to the Gulf. Thus, to the extent that one is looking for indications today as to Israel's relative importance to the United States, Israel's muted role in the Gulf conflict merely confirms that this is not objectively a key consideration.

Nevertheless, the Gulf War did become an important perceptual indicator of Israel's role in United States defense planning, both in the public's mind and in official circles. Yitzhak Rabin recalls that he spoke to a group of American college students during the fall of 1990 when the US troop deployment to the Middle East was underway.[27] One student stood up, remarked that her brother was in the Gulf, noted Israel's strength and the fact that Israel was a friend and ally of the United States, and asked Rabin, "Where are you?" What this wrenching question underscored for Rabin is the basic contradiction between US aid and its commitment to Israel on the one hand, and the fact that Israel's strength is often not considered usable in real-life contexts, on the other.

This grappling with the impact of US-Israeli strategic cooperation for the Gulf extended to official circles. At the outset of the war, both American and Israeli officials insisted that strategic cooperation had nothing to do with the Gulf crisis. As late as December 1990, Prime Minister Shamir, when asked about strategic cooperation, replied that because of the special characteristics of the war, and particularly the Arab coalition, the conflict did not fall into the realm of strategic cooperation.[28]

But with the start of the war, the enhanced cooperation that developed between the US and Israel clearly was integrated into the framework of strategic cooperation. Defense Ministry Director General David Ivry, Israeli chairman of the JPMG, said in early February 1991 that ongoing collaboration was "a good example of the essence of strategic cooperation."[29] Later that month, Prime Minister Shamir reported that he had "very amicable" talks with President Bush regarding strategic cooperation between the two countries, "especially everything concerning the current conflict."[30]

At a minimum, this slide of strategic cooperation into long-forbidden areas in 1991 says something important about the conceptual framework that undergirded the program for the preceding eight years. Almost without notice, the longstanding US preoccupation with separating Israel completely from the Arab states began to whither. For one, it became clear that such separation was not possible. Even if the United States does everything possible to keep Israel away from the rest of the region, the rest of the region will insist on pulling Israel in. Moreover, the war seemed to demonstrate that, under unique conditions, the Arab countries were willing both to turn a blind eye to quiet American-Israeli cooperation that did not involve any direct military role for Israel, and to accept the legitimacy of American and Israeli actions directed toward ensuring Israel's defense. Translated into implications for strategic cooperation, the following emerges: To the extent that strategic cooperation is directed primarily at ensuring Israel's legitimate defense, this is not a significant problem for most Arab states. However, to the extent that strategic cooperation is directed toward affecting events in the region as a whole, this will be more controversial. Perhaps the key criteria for what, in that case, would be acceptable or not are visibility, and whether one could trace a direct line from US-Arab cooperation to US-Israeli cooperation.

The one contingency that was never tested was whether the Arab coalition partners might have also accepted direct or indirect Israeli military assistance against a common enemy. Throughout the conflict, the US adamantly refused to coordinate with Israel on a possible Israeli retaliatory strike against Iraq. We will perhaps never know if this was a line drawn as a result of Washington's perception of what the Arabs would find unacceptable — or as a result of an explicit demand from the Arabs themselves. In any event, the lasting impression is likely to have reinforced the belief, at least for now, that there are clear and real limitations on Israeli involvement in a conflict involving the Arabs — even if it happens to be a conflict where Israel is under attack by an Arab state.[31]

Part III

Chapter 9. Looking to the Future

Breaking Old Taboos

In the months after the Gulf War, America's two top defense leaders reaffirmed the US-Israeli strategic relationship in some of the strongest terms used to date. Chairman of the Joint Chiefs General Colin Powell stated in a speech that the special friendship was "symbolized by the strategic cooperation between both countries, cooperation that benefits both of our countries, cooperation that will continue, cooperation that will grow."[1]

Defense Secretary Cheney went even further, stressing that US-Israeli cooperation prior to and during the Gulf War "contributed significantly to the success of the allied effort against Iraq."[2] He also noted that the entire Gulf experience was "a demonstration of the value of maintaining Israel's strength, and her ability to defend herself, and also the value of the strategic cooperation between our two countries."[3] This message was reinforced during Cheney's visit to Israel in May 1991, his first since becoming defense secretary.

This high-level praise for Israel was buttressed by decisions that, over time, will strengthen aspects of the strategic cooperation program. In May 1991, formal agreement was reached on the funding of the second stage of the Israeli Arrow ATBM program, with the United States covering 72 percent or about $300 million of the second phase costs, and Israel picking up the other 28 percent. Also, it was announced that the US would provide Israel with ten used F-15-A fighters, worth about $65 million, as part of a special $700 million allotment authorized for Israel by Congress the previous October. Up to that point, the administration had not acted to implement that authorization.

Of greatest significance, Cheney announced at the end of his visit to Israel that the US was in the process of prepositioning significant stockpiles of military equipment there for use in any conflict in the region.[4] While American and Israeli officials had secretly reached agreement years earlier to stockpile military equipment, and reinforced bunkers and storage areas had already been built in Israel, Cheney's announcement was the first high-level statement affirming that the program was indeed underway and was considered important to US military planners.

This increase in the program's visibility testifies to a certain breakdown in the taboos that have traditionally burdened closer US-Israeli strategic cooperation. No longer are American policymakers — particularly military officials — reluctant to talk openly about strategic cooperation, either because of hostility to the program or for fear of alienating the Arab world. Indeed, Cheney's announcement about prepositioning in Israel — long considered one of the most sensitive aspects of strategic cooperation — came as he prepared to fly on to Egypt.

This approach seems to stem, in the first instance, from the US desire to bolster Israeli deterrence and to counter any lingering impression from the Gulf War that US interests have shifted away from Israel toward the Arab world. By talking openly about strategic cooperation, US officials further underscore to any potential aggressor — as well as to an always nervous Israeli public — the American commitment to Israel's security.

Of even greater fundamental significance, the more relaxed and open US approach to discussing the program reflects the evolution of strategic cooperation from a controversial issue to "just another" aspect of US-Israeli bilateral relations, widely accepted even if not always liked. Even long-time critics of strategic cooperation acknowledge the importance of maintaining a strong US commitment to Israel's security, of which strategic cooperation is perceived to be an integral part. Any effort to dismantle the program — were it to be interpreted as a lessening of US support for Israel — could have dangerous consequences, both for Israel's deterrent posture and for stability in the Middle East. As one sceptic of strategic cooperation noted, "We're stuck with a strong, solid relationship with Israel."[5]

Directions for the Future

But if strategic cooperation has become an accepted part of the political landscape, the future shape of the program is far from certain as we look toward the next century. Strategic cooperation was essentially a compromise formula developed by the Reagan

Administration to fill the middle ground between a formal agreement, such as a defense treaty, and the absence of any overarching program at all — which is what Secretary of Defense Weinberger would have preferred.

As we look to the future, it is certainly possible to envision changes in the strategic cooperation program — toward either greater or less formalization. The idea of a defense treaty periodically crops up, usually in connection with American efforts to encourage Israel to be more forthcoming in the peace process. While not referring specifically to a defense treaty, President Bush spoke in March 1991 of the need to find ways "where we can kind of help guarantee" Israel's security requirements.[6] Thus, one possible evolution of strategic cooperation might be in the direction of creating a binding set of obligations that would require the US to come to Israel's aid under defined situations. However, the only conceivable circumstances under which such commitments might be given would involve a comprehensive Israeli-Arab peace.

Another way that strategic cooperation could take on greater significance over the next ten years would be for the US to assign, in practical terms, a role for Israel in American defense planning for the region. This Washington has long been reluctant to do because of the Arab states. It might mean including Israel in a single US command encompassing the region (erasing the artificial boundaries between EUCOM and CENTCOM), or it might simply mean establishing more informal and tacit forms of cooperation with Israel in the region, including American use of Israeli facilities in the event of another major regional conflict. Cheney's announcement regarding the prepositioning of war materiel in Israel for use in the region could be seen as a step in this direction.

Alternatively, it is also possible that strategic cooperation could be cut back quietly in the years ahead, or effectively stripped of genuine meaning. While this is not likely to include a diminution in the stated US commitment to Israel's security or a repudiation of the overall concept of strategic cooperation, it could result in reduced "fringe benefits" for Israel in the form of fewer monetary advantages (reduced off-shore procurement and construction projects, etc.) or a wholesale cutback in the number of US exercises in, or ship visits to, Israel.

Whether strategic cooperation moves in the direction of expansion or contraction will depend on three central considerations: a) how the United States defines its strategic interests in the Middle East in the future; b) what military requirements and capabilities the US will need in the region, and, most important, c) whether there is the political will in the United States to expand cooperation with Israel.

Strategic interests

It seems safe to assume that the United States will continue to have very important strategic interests in the Middle East (including the Persian Gulf) at least through the end of this century. The Gulf War underscored the prime US interest in ensuring oil supplies from the region. By the end of this century, experts predict that the West will be even more dependent on Persian Gulf oil supplies.

Another abiding strategic interest of the US has been the maintenance of "strategic stability" in the region, i.e., the prevention of war. As the region becomes saturated with ever-sophisticated weapons and missiles, the stakes of any potential future conflict — for players in and outside the Middle East — will continue to rise. One of the reasons support for Israel is likely to remain an important part of US strategic calculations in the area, in addition to American domestic sympathy with Israel, is that a strong Israel is an important condition for strategic stability in the region.

Thus, even without traditional US concern about countering the Soviets, it seems safe to assume that the US will regard the Middle East as a strategically important place. Indeed, the US may see the diminution of Soviet influence as an opportunity finally to consolidate American leverage throughout the region. Moreover, because US military planners will remain preoccupied with the task of defending the Persian Gulf oilfields, American thinking about the region will continue to be shaped by contingency plans for the possible use of force in the future.

Military requirements

But if the US military is likely to remain actively engaged in the area, it is less clear whether this will translate into greater cooperation with Israel. One key factor affecting strategic cooperation will be American success in gaining access elsewhere in the region. As noted earlier, in this regard Israel has presented two main drawbacks from the perspective of US military planners: its physical distance from the oilfields, and its seeming incompatibility with the Arab world. If the US finds ready access in the Arab world and Persian Gulf region itself, it will be less interested in looking seriously at potential options in Israel. However, to the extent that the Arab countries are less than forthcoming about future contingency arrangements, Israel becomes potentially more attractive. Also, looking further ahead, any widespread destabilization in the Arab world would also tend to increase the relative value of Israel.

Certainly with the United States playing a more active direct military role in the region, there will likely be a host of new military requirements in support of US objectives. In the aftermath of the Gulf War Washington may have to consider reorganizing EUCOM and CENTCOM in order to facilitate future American operations in the Eastern Mediterranean and the Gulf. This could break down barriers that currently determine where US POMCUS stocks are prepositioned,[7] where the US can use beddown facilities for its aircraft in a crisis, and the requirements for staging bases and related storage facilities.

Another key factor affecting strategic cooperation from the American military perspective will be the issue of scarce resources. Over the five-year period from 1991 to 1996, the armed services are to shrink by about 25 percent in response to federal budget pressures and the decline of the Soviet Union as a global adversary. As American bases are closed, US assembly lines dismantled, and thousands of American jobs lost, Israel will face an extremely tough and critical environment for its own aid requests. This has already produced extreme sensitivity among congressmen and women facing reelection in districts where bases and defense plants are being shut down, with regard to the perception of scarce resources being diverted from domestic needs. Though Israel's 1991 request for $10 billion in loan guarantees did not actually require a major outlay of funds from the US government, even the perception that the US has $10 billion to invest outside of the country is very sensitive.

Without a doubt, a 25 percent defense budget reduction will eventually cut into nearly every aspect of the US military budget, including strategic cooperation — which, regardless of what the US gets in return, does indeed cost money. The Defense Attache Office in Israel is one of the largest in the world, having grown tenfold since the early 1980s and now receiving more than a thousand visitors per year.[8] Major exercises involving Israeli forces cost individual American services a lot of money. The building of ammunition storage bunkers and the supply of $300 million in prepositioned equipment costs money. Ship visits in Israel leave behind over $1 million per day. As one American military officer noted, even a ten percent reduction in assistance to, or programs with Israel could save a lot of smaller programs elsewhere abroad.[9]

On the other hand, the US military effort to become more efficient and streamlined could also positively affect Israeli defense industries. On the whole, the need for cooperative R&D projects will not decrease in the new strategic environment. Moreover, as policymakers are forced to cancel planned projects and turn instead to modernizing existing platforms, Israel can contribute a great deal based on its own experience in upgrading platforms.[10] US interest in Israeli technology, already evident in their SDI cooperation, thus should continue as US defense policy remains preoccupied with technological improvement.[11]

There is thus no hard and fast bottom line regarding the military's need for greater or reduced strategic cooperation in the future. The military as a whole, as a tradition-bound institution, is more likely than not to follow previously-decided guidelines. Perhaps the most that can be said is that there will be pressures to marginally increase strategic cooperation in some areas and to marginally decrease it in others. But a wholesale expansion of the program would probably only follow the collapse of US plans for cooperation with the Arab states.

Political will

The third and most important factor that will affect strategic cooperation in the future is what might be termed "political will" in Washington. The key consideration for the commencement of effective strategic cooperation in 1983 was not military but political; it should come as no surprise today that any major changes in the program would also stem from political or political-strategic considerations.

Political will stems from several sources. One is the way the administration looks at the issue. Here it seems clear that, in addition to domestic political considerations, administration decisionmaking rests on a perception on the part of key policymakers as to the way in which greater or lesser support for Israel will affect US objectives in the region as a whole. It is important to recall that at key junctures in the past, US decisions regarding Israel were heavily influenced by the administration's strategic analysis of conditions in the region. Thus, Nixon and Kissinger intervened in the 1973 war in large part because they believed that would best serve US strategic interests in the region. In 1983, a strong reason for moving ahead with strategic cooperation was the administration's frustration with the Arab countries and its calculation that strengthening US-Israeli cooperation would serve its broader strategic interests in the area.

Thus, one of the key considerations affecting an administration decision to curtail or expand strategic cooperation is its analysis of how that would affect other US interests in the region. One consideration, already alluded to, is the US concern to preserve strategic stability in the region. This argues against any radical reduction in strategic cooperation. On the other hand, another key US objective is to foster progress on the peace front; it is constantly looking for subtle levers that could be used to this end. While we have not yet seen strategic cooperation used as a "stick" — i.e., curtailed as an incentive toward compromising for peace — it definitely does seem to be a "carrot," in that it would doubtless be expanded as part of the "payoff" for progress toward a peace agreement.

Political will also derives from popular American support for

Israel. Without a doubt, this provides the key parameter within which the administration must operate. While strategic rationales have come and gone, what has continued to undergird strategic cooperation is the basic American commitment to maintaining a special friendship with Israel based on the unique moral, democratic and cultural bonds that exist between the two countries.

This is manifested in congressional support for Israel. As has been pointed out several times in the course of this study, Congress directly affects aid levels to Israel that constitute one very important aspect of strategic cooperation. In those few instances in the past 20 years when the administration has sought to withhold aid from Israel, it has been to Congress that Israeli supporters have turned.

Thus, any sign that popular support for Israel may be eroding is cause for genuine concern, both because of the potential ripple effect on Congress and because of the administration's perception of the pressures it can exert on Israel given political realities. Prior to the Gulf War we witnessed for the first time support in Congress for reducing aid to Israel. Even though this did not occur — indeed, following the outbreak of war Congress approved two supplemental appropriations for Israel — there is also growing frustration in Congress with Israel's settlement policy in the Territories, which is seen as an obstacle to peace. As Israel seeks $10 billion in loan guarantees to settle new Soviet immigrants, it may find the environment on Capitol Hill less sympathetic than any it has encountered for many years.

Without a doubt, the Palestinian uprising and Israel's policies toward the Arab population under its control, amplified by the media, have had an effect on American public opinion toward Israel. The fact that a group of Jewish Democrats have felt compelled to form an organization aimed at battling in the party for Jewish causes underscores subtle changes that are taking place in the American political scene. In this case, the Jewish organizers were alarmed at a spate of anti-Israel (and pro-Palestinian) resolutions offered at various state Democratic Party conventions during the 1988 presidential campaign.[12]

Were Israel to appear to be no longer committed to the values that drew American support in the first place, it is highly doubtful that strategic relations between the two countries could sustain the relationship at its present high level. General Powell, in his aforementioned speech, went so far as to refer to the "democratic cooperation" and the "moral cooperation" that existed between the US and Israel prior to strategic cooperation, and which remain integral to the strategic relationship.[13]

Here, then, the focus is upon the centrality of the peace issue. This is the single most important issue affecting political will, hence support for strategic cooperation. Israel's approach to peace is not only an important part of American public perceptions of Israel, it has become a very real policy issue affecting the administration's view of Israel. US officials have long seen strength and peace as two sides of the same coin; top Defense officials reaffirmed this connection in no uncertain terms after the Gulf War.[14]

One of the main reasons that peace is such an important issue for strategic cooperation is that, without peace, the US has to try constantly to juggle competing interests with Israel and with the Arab world. This elementary equation underlines the premise that one of the key factors limiting strategic cooperation through the years has been American reluctance to be seen to be collaborating with Israel in the region.

Practically speaking, peace is the watershed issue that will determine whether strategic cooperation is significantly expanded in terms of aid and commitments. Certainly, when there has been demonstrable progress on the peace front, US aid has followed in its wake. One senior American diplomat envisioned that, as part of an arrangement on the Palestinian issue, the US would end up investing billions of dollars to make it work: in demilitarization arrangements, intelligence and verification, water-sharing arrangements, financial support for the parties, and so on. The effect for cooperation between the two sides would obviously be dramatic — as important as the Israeli-Egyptian peace agreement was at the beginning of the 1980s.

In the absence of peace, particularly should Israel be perceived as an obstacle, it is hard to envision a US decision to significantly expand US-Israeli strategic cooperation. Indeed, the administration may well look to the strategic cooperation agreement for quiet ways to show its displeasure about Israeli policies. Without actually reducing annual aid to Israel, the administration could bow to budget pressures that are already building up, to cut back on training exercises with Israel, ship visits, and even prepositioning.

Clearly the interaction between the peace process and strategic cooperation with Israel presents Washington with a dilemma. In the past, it was argued that if Israel were confident about its security and about US support, it would be able to make tough decisions on the question of peace. While this assumption was seriously called into question by events between 1988 and 1991, as one senior American diplomat noted, there certainly is no evidence to suggest that an insecure Israel, one that had lost confidence in the US, would make moves toward peace. As one observer put it, the recurring pattern in Middle East politics appears to be, "When I am weak, how can I compromise? When I am strong, why should I compromise?"[15]

The Lost Soviet Rationale

Absent thus far from our discussion of the factors that will affect strategic cooperation in the future is that longstanding rationale for cooperation with Israel: countering the Soviet threat. Its disappearance is all the more striking when one considers how instrumental the Soviet threat had been in fostering closer US-Israeli cooperation through the years: under Nixon and Kissinger, Israel became an asset because of the Soviet presence in the region; Reagan's open embrace of Israel and the later codification of a strategic relationship was justified on the basis of the Soviet threat. Not only did it provide an important rationale to use with the Arabs, it also served to identify an explicit strategic role for Israel, specifically in the Eastern Mediterranean.

Now, as a concept, it is gone. Early in the Bush Administration some effort was made to grapple with the problem and to justify strategic cooperation using vaguer, broader rationales. Remarks by Defense Minister Cheney and Under Secretary Wolfowitz to this end were previously noted. More recently, Deputy Secretary Eagleburger, when asked about the purpose of strategic cooperation in the post-Cold War era, responded that "it serves the general purpose of providing a close link between the United States and Israel for any number of contingencies. Obviously problems in and around this area would be a part of that process."[16]

The ease with which Washington has adjusted to losing its primary rationale for strategic cooperation says something important about what, for it, is the real point of cooperation with Israel. Yes, strategic cooperation was born of a lingering belief that, on that giant chessboard of superpower competition, Israel could help to improve the American position in one critical area of competition, the Middle East. But there was also the hope that a strong and confident Israel would be more willing to take risks for peace and to be more responsive to American requirements in the region. And there were the pressures that stemmed from domestic politics at home. Finally, there were the unalterable facts of Israel's strength in the region, the special friendship between the two countries, and the amount of aid that was pouring into Israel on an annual basis.

It is this complex mix of motivations for strategic cooperation that serves as its greatest protection. Because there was no one imperative for strategic cooperation, there will likely never be one reason for its decline. Strategic cooperation exists, in the final analysis, because an extremely close US-Israeli relationship exists.

In this sense it is significant that, with the implementation of strategic cooperation starting in 1984, the Soviet rationale quickly faded as an issue of direct relevance for the program. The Israelis were not happy linking everything to the Soviets, and the US was not facing a genuine military requirement for Israeli assistance. Hence both sides quickly turned their attention to more practical manifestations of strategic cooperation. Thus, by the time the Cold War was said to be over, the residual effect of the early preoccupation with the Soviets was largely a matter of ritual, not of practice. Meanwhile, with or without the excuse of the Soviet threat, the Arabs had come grudgingly to accept strategic cooperation as part of the landscape.

No one interviewed for this research effort, either American or Israeli, attached any significance to the fading of the Soviet threat for strategic cooperation. As one former American official drily noted, in general, the less seriously people took the Soviet threat in the mid-1980s, the more they insisted on including it in the rationale for the program.[17] Another official, in agreeing with this dictum, commented that most Americans who supported strategic cooperation during the Cold War still support it now.[18] Meanwhile, the officials insist, the Soviet threat is not completely gone; even if it were, there are plenty of other threats to be concerned about. Indeed, one may argue that the very collapse of the Soviet Union offers new rationales for American-Israeli (and even Russian) strategic cooperation, e.g., in coping with the behavior of the Muslim Central Asian republics of the former Soviet Union.

The Legacy of Strategic Cooperation

The legacy of strategic cooperation is a strangely mixed one. First, even though controversy continues to exist about strategic cooperation among experts in Washington, the very nature of the debate has changed irrevocably. Twenty, even ten years ago, when people argued about whether Israel had any value for the United States, at stake were actual decisions affecting US moves toward closer cooperation with Israel at the perceived expense of American interests in the Arab world. Today, strategic cooperation with Israel has become so well established that the assertion that Israel has no strategic value is, to a large degree, a non sequitur. Israel has strategic value if for no other reason than the fact that the US is so committed to it.

Secondly, while American officials interviewed for this research effort drew attention to the real benefits that the US derives from the program, they also all said that the US could live without strategic cooperation. True, American participants appreciate Israel's dependability and military capabilities, its intelligence-sharing and technology transfer, and America's access to facilities in Israel — including the use of bombing ranges in the Negev, airbases built as a consequence of the Camp David agreements, and the Port of Haifa. And Americans evince considerable respect for their Israeli counterparts. That said, strategic cooperation does not seem to fill some essential gap in US security planning.

This dichotomy is reflected in the way US officials, such as Defense Secretary Cheney and JCS Chairman Powell, talk about the issue. Even while expressing strong support for strategic cooperation with Israel, neither of them has described Israel as a key player in US defense planning, or as having an important military role to play in defending US interests in the region. Rather, the focus of their comments is on the need for a strong Israel — for deterrence, to protect itself, and for peace.

These comments, then, underscore the importance of looking at strategic cooperation in the context of the total US-Israeli relationship. Yes, the program is firmly established, but only within the context of the US-Israeli relationship — not within some independent determination of US national interests. Thus strategic cooperation should not be considered immune from the broader US-Israeli relationship. If the latter were to teeter, there is no reason to expect that strategic cooperation would somehow emerge unscathed.

The third mixed legacy of strategic cooperation is in the practical implementation of the program. Even though Israel is widely seen in the US as a stabilizing force in the region and as a friend that can be counted on in an emergency, officials on both sides have difficulty coming up with examples of where strategic cooperation, in the sense of actual US and Israeli military collaboration, might be put to the test. US-Israeli cooperation in 1970 during the Jordan crisis continues to stand as the clearest example of collaboration in action. While there are plenty of examples of technological cooperation (e.g., SDI) or covert cooperation (Iran-Contra), more often than not the US has not been willing to be seen as openly collaborating with Israel in the region.

Participants in the program recognize as well as anyone else how problematic it is to define a specific strategic role for Israel. As a former senior Israeli participant noted, the issue of whether strategic cooperation was about the US and Israel cooperating in the region, or, rather, cooperating on behalf of Israel's defense, was simply never resolved.[19] The predominant view was that a strong Israel was an essential player in the regional picture. It didn't go beyond this.

Thus, while officials from both sides tend to present strategic cooperation as helping to improve their ability to act in a variety of situations that might arise in the Middle East, the question of whether either country would *choose* to cooperate with the other, or to take joint action, is a different issue. Clearly it would depend on the particular situation and the perception of Israel at the time. As officials emphasize, there is absolutely nothing mechanical about strategic cooperation that would obligate either side to coordinate with the other. Several American officials note that the US never envisioned using Israeli troops in the region anyway.

In the meantime, the US clearly recognizes Israel's tacit role in maintaining stability in the region, particularly with regard to Jordan where, since at least 1970, Israel's "red line" regarding the intervention of any outside forces must be taken into account by any potential aggressor. US officials also mention Israel's role in counter-terrorism (which has not been discussed in this work), and in other "unconventional" areas such as drug trafficking.

Finally, strategic cooperation generates a mixed legacy for anyone trying to define the US commitment to Israel's security. Although strategic cooperation was a compromise formula that fell short of a defense treaty, the reality of strategic cooperation has resulted in nearly everything one would find in a treaty, but without any formal obligations and without the presence of US troops on Israel's soil. Basically, the thrust of strategic cooperation through the years has been to ensure the defense of Israel. Crisis resupply, the prepositioning of equipment in Israel, training and joint exercises — all have resulted in a generic ability of both sides to react quickly in a crisis. The quick deployment of the Patriot batteries to Israel in the initial days of the Gulf War underscores how close this relationship had become and how effectively it was tailored to a "real world" crisis situation.

The one key aspect that strategic cooperation has not solved is the necessity for a political decision at any given time to trigger the necessary coordination. As Zeev Schiff has pointed out vividly, there are many different scenarios whereby it is not at all certain that the US would automatically side with Israel and thus quickly come to its defense.[20]

Nor is there any certainty that a defense treaty would solve this issue either. A treaty would likely continue to circumscribe the conditions under which an "automatic" response would be forthcoming. Moreover, one of the primary lessons for Israel of Iraq's invasion of Kuwait was not, as many Americans saw it, the enhancement of American credibility in the region, but rather the inability of the US to deploy an effective force to the region in under three months, as well as Washington's ineffectual postwar treatment of the Kurdish issue. Thus for Israel the issue is not simply whether the US would respond, but whether the response would be timely.

Were US troops to be stationed in Israel, response time would presumably be significantly reduced and the deterrent value of the US commitment would grow correspondingly. But any US deployment would raise a new set of problems from Israel's perspective — problems related to its sovereignty and control over its own destiny. It is for these reasons that many Israeli officials would prefer that additional American assurances to Israel include not political commitments, but rather additional aid, prepositioned stocks, and practical forms of cooperation such as the early-warning system established during the Gulf War but then dismantled. It is these practical forms of cooperation, as Rabin and other Israeli officials point out, that give Israel the capability to defend itself.

Finally, with regard to the value of formal versus informal American commitments, as we have seen so vividly over the last few years, even bedrock security commitments such as NATO can change in light of new security conditions. Yet this does not necessarily change the American perception of where its sympathies or obligations lie. Taiwan is the perfect case in point. A number of years ago, in the face of overbearing strategic interests regarding China, the US walked away from a formal relationship with Taiwan. But far from diluting its longstanding sympathy for Taiwan, Washington has continued to maintain a very important defense relationship there, and an important role in Taiwan's deterrent vis-a-vis the PRC, as well as promoting PRC-Taiwanese rapprochement. This stems not from any formal obligation, but rather from a sense of moral obligation.

US Ambassador to Israel William Brown has noted that the US is one of the few countries in the world to view its alliances or obligations with real sincerity.[21] Although it may not always appear that way to the rest of the world, American foreign policy — particularly in the last 20 years — has been affected by a popular desire to do the morally right thing; to support forces overseas that are perceived to be on the side of good.

The bottom line for strategic cooperation is that it rests on this greater foundation of US interests, loyalties and morality. The US-Israeli relationship has been supported by the perception that Israel shares so many basic characteristics with America: its struggle for democracy, its Judeo-Christian values, and its historical heritage. At both the top and at the working level, Americans have most often been able to find common ground with Israelis and to identify with them. Here it bears emphasis that there is a real danger should Israel no longer be perceived in this way. From Ferdinand Marcos to Manuel Noriega to the attempted hardline takeover in Moscow in August 1991, Americans do not like supporting those who appear to be oppressors.

More or Less Strategic Cooperation?

Very real limits exist today on the curtailment or expansion of strategic cooperation. Curtailment would clearly be destabilizing in a regional context, and would be punitive for both the US and Israel, given the very real benefits that flow from the program. No one interviewed, either American or Israeli, could envision a time when some type of cooperation in the defense realm would cease to exist between the two countries. Even were the US to manipulate the margins of strategic cooperation so as to exert pressure on Israeli policies, everyone agreed that this should stop well short of anything that might jeopardize Israel's security. The $1.8 billion in military aid is essential, the additional sources perhaps not.

Expansion of the program is limited by the absence of conditions whereby the US is willing to be seen as collaborating with Israel. In other words, until and unless the US is willing to get more back from the program through more effective use of Israeli facilities and resources to further American military objectives in the region, there is little point in contemplating an escalation in military cooperation.

This suggests that the central weakness of strategic cooperation as it presently exists is not in the military realm but in the political parameters within which the US is willing to use it: Washington has traditionally been reluctant to be seen collaborating with Israel in the region. This reluctance used to stem from official US concern about alienating the Arab countries. While this official concern has diminished somewhat over the years, the US continues carefully to weigh the potential costs against any benefits of cooperating with Israel. Meanwhile, unease has been growing within the United States over Israel's stance on the peace process, and specifically with its treatment of the Palestinian population.

Thus the successful military-to-military relationship that has been established tends to flow in vacuum because it is not backed up by a broader political dialogue as to what strategic cooperation should be achieving for both sides. The Joint Political-Military Group, or JPMG, began as an effort to provide the political context for the relationship. But as the years went by, both sides focused increasingly on the wealth of details associated with dispensing a large aid program and overseeing their diverse and far-reaching cooperation in various technical fields. Today, with the JPMG only meeting once or twice a year and no longer addressing the broader issues in the relationship, the state of dialogue between the two sides is surprisingly weak.

One way to correct this would be the creation of a new forum to address the political side of strategic cooperation. Such a policy-oriented group could meet at regularly-scheduled times to discuss the fundamentally political issues that now receive much less attention than the strictly military-to-military questions.

One obvious starting point is to examine whether strategic cooperation needs to be reexamined in light of the changes that have taken place in the Soviet Union. As emphasized throughout this work, the loss of the Soviet threat does not shake the foundations of strategic cooperation. As many of those interviewed emphasized, strategic cooperation is not scenario dependent and thus can be used in any context. Still, the written scenarios that are a part of strategic cooperation are indeed Soviet-oriented. Moreover, the changes that have taken place both with regard to the Soviet Union and in the wake of the Gulf War offer a unique opportunity for the US and Israel to rethink the objectives that strategic cooperation should be serving for both sides. This does not require the identification of specific threats. But if US military planners are trying to fashion a new security regime for the region into the next century, this is the time for an ongoing dialogue between the two sides as to how US-Israeli cooperation might serve that end.

We noted at the outset that there is no "correct" view of what strategic cooperation is all about. In its broadest sense, it means different things to different people. If there is any residue of controversy about strategic cooperation, it is over the nagging question of why the relationship should be called "strategic." Some Americans have always resented this aspect of the program, feeling that the entire concept has been hyped and oversold through the years.

The maturity of the relationship today transcends that issue. Perhaps one Israeli official put it best when he said that he preferred to refer to the breadth of ties that had developed as "defense relations" rather than strategic cooperation, because this term was less pretentious and conveyed more meaning as to the reality of the program. As both sides consider strategic cooperation — or defense relations — through the end of this century, they can be pleased with a legacy that, leaving aside the theoretical debates and ideological hype, has clearly proven its value.

Notes

Chapter 1

[1] For particularly good accounts of US policy toward Israel during these early years, see Peter Grose, *Israel In the Mind of America* (New York: Alfred A. Knopf, 1983), and Steven L. Spiegel, *The Other Arab-Israeli Conflict* (University of Chicago Press, 1985).
[2] Spiegel, *ibid.*, p. 54.
[3] Grose, *Israel in the Mind*, p. 303.
[4] Spiegel, *The Other Conflict*, p. 51.
[5] I. L. Kenen, *Israel's Defense Line* (Prometheus Books, 1981), p. 88.
[6] Kenen, *ibid.*, p. 130.
[7] For a succinct account of arms sales to Israel in the 1960s see Mitchell G. Bard, "The Turning Point in US Relations with Israel," *Middle East Review*, Summer 1988, pp. 50-57.
[8] William B. Quandt, *Decade of Decisions: American Policy Toward the Arab-Israeli Conflict* (University of California Press, 1977), p. 61.
[9] Grose, *Israel in the Mind*, pp. 309-310.
[10] Shai Feldman, *US Middle East Policy: The Domestic Setting*, JCSS Special Study (Westview Press, 1988), p. 35.
[11] Spiegel, *The Other Conflict*, p. 161.
[12] Spiegel notes that President Johnson did not need much coaxing from Congress since he was already leaning in the direction of selling the planes to Israel, but that he first wanted to explore Soviet willingness to cooperate on limiting arms to the region. See pages 160-164.
[13] Chaim Herzog, *The Arab-Israeli Wars* (New York: Vintage Books, 1984), p. 196.
[14] Bard, "Turning Point," pp. 55-56.
[15] See Spiegel, pp. 168-69 on the effects of the Jewish lobby on the Nixon Administration. While Nixon boasted that he was not beholden to Jewish interests, in fact, Spiegel argues that Nixon was not immune from political pressures on this issue, particularly as he became weaker as a result of Watergate.
[16] Henry Kissinger, *White House Years* (Boston: Little, Brown, 1979), p. 563.
[17] Yitzhak Rabin, *The Rabin Memoirs* (Boston: Little, Brown, 1979), pp. 187. Marvin and Bernard Kalb also claim that the request for Israeli intervention came from King Hussein. Marvin and Bernard Kalb, *Kissinger* (Boston: Little, Brown, 1974), p. 202. Kissinger asserts in his memoirs, however, that the request was an American one.
[18] Kissinger, *White House Years*, pp. 594-631.
[19] *Ibid.*, p. 607 and p. 622.
[20] Rabin, *Memoirs*, p. 188.
[21] Interview with Yitzhak Rabin, December 12, 1990.

[22] Rabin recounts that a group of American officers took off from one of the carriers and came to Israel to discuss operational coordination. *Memoirs*, p. 184.
[23] *Ibid.*, p. 189.
[24] Kissinger, *White House Years*, p. 631.
[25] Kalb, *Kissinger*, p. 208.
[26] Itamar Rabinovich, "Israel and the Western Alliance," *The Middle East and the Western Alliance*, ed. by Steven L. Spiegel (Allen & Unwin, 1982), p. 200.
[27] Rabin, *Memoirs*, p. 189.
[28] Abba Eban interview, *Jerusalem Post* Supplement, July 4, 1984, p. VII.
[29] Spiegel, *The Other Conflict*, p. 202.
[30] Interview with Ambassador Samuel Lewis, October 2, 1990.
[31] Spiegel, *The Other Conflict*, p. 256.
[32] Transcript of news conference by Kissinger, November 12, 1973.
[33] Quandt, *Decade*, p. 170.
[34] Henry Kissinger, *Years of Upheaval* (Boston: Little, Brown, 1982), p. 602.
[35] *Ibid*, p. 493.
[36] The $2.2 billion was approved by unheard of margins, specifically 66 to 9 in the Senate, and 364 to 52 in the House. Kenen, *Defense Line*, p. 306.
[37] Kissinger, *Upheaval*, p. 483.
[38] Spiegel's book contains several striking quotations from U.S. officials, such as JCS Chairman George Brown, which were highly critical of Israel and openly opposed to a closer bilateral relationship. See p. 221, also pp. 234 and 251.
[39] Quandt, *Decade*, p. 202.
[40] Indeed, some in Israel believe that certain Pentagon officials delayed beginning the airlift so as to "bleed" Israel first, thereby making Israel more in need of aid and therefore more prepared to submit to US political demands during later negotiations.
[41] *Israel's Foreign Relations* (hereafter *IFR*), Selected Documents, 1974-1977, Meron Medzini, editor (Jerusalem: Ministry of Foreign Affairs, 1982), p. 152.
[42] *Ibid.*, p. 306.
[43] Jimmy Carter, *Keeping Faith: Memoirs of a President* (Toronto; New York: Bantam Books, 1982), p. 414.
[44] According to Charles Kupchan, some voices in the Carter Administration called for closer military ties with Israel, including more Israeli involvement in basing schemes for the RDF. Paul Wolfowitz was one of the principal figures. Charles A. Kupchan, *The Persian Gulf and the West: Dilemmas of Security* (Allen & Unwin, 1987), p. 136 and notes.
[45] *IFR*, p. 536.
[46] See *IFR*, 1974-1977, pp. 287-290 for the documents.
[47] See *American Foreign Policy, Basic Documents* (hereafter *AFP*), 1977-1980, pp. 684-685 for the MOAs; see p. 667 for the Brown letter to Weizman; and see pp. 699-700 and 713-715 for

further agreements related to US supply of oil to Israel.

[48] For a complete analysis of US-Israeli cooperation in defense-industrial fields, see Dore Gold, *Israel as an American Non-NATO Ally*, JCSS Study no. 19 (Boulder: Westview Press, forthcoming 1992).

[49] See Kissinger's and Peres' remarks on September 20, 1975 as well as Prime Minister Rabin's statement to the Knesset on February 9, 1976. *IFR*, pp. 311-312 and pp. 441-444.

[50] Based on interviews with Israeli officials including Dr. Elyakim Rubinstein (January 10, 1991), Major General (ret.) Menachem Meron (December 11, 1990) and Brigadier General (ret.) Mordechai Zippori (January 3, 1991).

[51] Interview with Mordechai Zippori, January 3, 1991.

Chapter 2

[1] Specifically, Ronald Reagan stated in an August 15, 1979 *Washington Post* op-ed piece that: "The fall of Iran has increased Israel's value as perhaps the only remaining strategic asset in the region on which the United States can truly rely." And, besides stating that Israel's facilities and airfields could provide the US with a secure point of access, Reagan also stated that "Soviet planners must constantly take into account the effective dominance of Israel's forces and especially its air force, over critical zones of access and transit in the region. In a moment of crisis...(this would) greatly restrict Soviet options and thereby facilitate the tasks of American planners." Cited in Toby Dershowitz, ed., *The Reagan Administration and Israel: Key Statements*. AIPAC Papers on US-Israeli Relations, 1987, pp. 3-6.
[2] For the texts of the convention platforms, as well as the positions of Anderson and Carter on Israel, see *Congressional Quarterly Weekly*, July 19, 1980, pp. 2053-54; August 16, 1980, pp. 2432 and 2412-13; and October 18, 1980, pp. 3159-60.
[3] *Ibid.*, July 19, 1980, p. 2054.
[4] See Dore Gold, *America, the Gulf and Israel*, JCSS Study no. 11 (Boulder: Westview Press, 1988) for a succinct analysis of the challenges facing US military planners at this time and of how the decision to become directly involved in defense of the region differed from previous US strategy for the area.
[5] See Jeffrey Record, *The Rapid Deployment Force and US Military Intervention in the Persian Gulf* (Institute for Policy Analysis, May 1983), Second Edition, p. 83.
[6] Joseph Churba, "The Eroding Security Balance in the Middle East," *Orbis*, Summer 1980, pp. 353-361.
[7] George W. Ball, "The Coming Crisis in Israeli-American Relations," *Foreign Affairs*, Winter 1979/1980, pp. 231-256.
[8] Alexander M. Haig, Jr., *Caveat* (New York: MacMillan Publishing Company, 1984), p. 170.
[9] During Haig's first meeting with Washington reporters, he stated that international terrorism would take the place of human rights as a central US concern. *Ibid.*, p. 194.
[10] Specifically, Begin stated: "I believe experience has proved that you cannot remedy a certain situation through bringing troops from afar. And therefore I support that the US should rely on its real allies and those that keep forces in the Middle East." *IFR*, 1979-80, p. 375. In another interview, Begin explicitly stated that if the US wanted facilities in Israel, "we shall put them at your disposal." *IFR*, 1979-80, pp. 236-241.
[11] Two examples can be found in *IFR*, 1981-82, #36 and #44. The first is a July 1981 interview with ABC, the second a statement to the Knesset in August 1981.
[12] *AFP*, 1981, #283, p. 657.
[13] Joe Stork, "Israel as a Strategic Asset," *MERIP Reports*, May 1982, p. 9.

[14] *New York Times*, October 1, 1981.
[15] Kupchan, *Dilemma of Security*, p. 144.
[16] *Ibid.*, p. 139.
[17] Haig, *Caveat*, pp. 179-80.
[18] *IFR*, 1981-82, #13, p. 38.
[19] *Jerusalem Post* International Edition, June 21-27, 1981, p. 1.
[20] See, for instance, the July 31, 1981 *Christian Science Monitor*, p. 1 which questioned what strategic benefits Israel conferred on the U.S.
[21] *IFR*, 1981-82, p. 143.
[22] Interview with Ambassador Samuel Lewis, October 2, 1990.
[23] *Yediot Aharonot*, September 28, 1981; *IFR*, 1981-82, pp. 152-158.
[24] *Jerusalem Post* International Edition, September 13-19, 1981, p. 1, or *Washington Post*, September 12, 1981.
[25] *IFR*, 1981-82, #55, pp. 141-142.
[26] See Major General Avraham Tamir, *A Soldier in Search of Peace*, edited by Joan Comay (New York: Harper & Row), particularly pp. 214-215.
[27] Zeev Schiff and Ehud Ya'ari, *Israel's Lebanon War*, updated edition, edited and translated by Iran Friedman (London: Unwin Paperbacks, 1986), pp. 62-63.
[28] *IFR*, 1981-82, #55, p. 142.
[29] Tamir, *Soldier*, p. 214.
[30] See *IFR*, 1981-82, #31, pp 84-89; an interview with *CBS*, #36, pp. 94-97; an interview with *ABC*, #43, pp. 105-114; and a Knesset statement, #44, pp. 114-119.
[31] *AFP*, Current Documents, 1981, p. 681.
[32] *Ibid.*, p. 674.
[33] *Jerusalem Post* International Edition, September 20-26, 1981, p. 1.
[34] See Ariel Sharon's own account of his presentations in his *Warrior* (New York: Simon and Schuster, 1989), pp. 412-413.
[35] *Ibid.*
[36] *Jerusalem Post* International Edition, September 20-26, 1981.
[37] Sharon, *Warrior*, p. 414.
[38] Interview with Major General Menachem Meron, December 11, 1990.
[39] Interview with former Assistant Secretary of State Nicholas Veliotes, December 18, 1990.
[40] *New York Times*, September 6, 1981, p. 1, or *Christian Science Monitor*, September 9, 1981, p. 1.
[41] *Jerusalem Post*, September 18, 1981, p. 16.
[42] *IFR*, 1981-82, #37, p. 98.
[43] Haig, *Caveat*, p. 190 and p. 328.
[44] Although the MOU did not explicitly cover intelligence exchanges between the two countries, these exchanges had continued uninterrupted since the early days and were generally regarded as being on a separate track from strategic cooperation.
[45] Haig, *Caveat*, p. 328.
[46] Sharon, *Warrior*, p. 414.

[47] *New York Times*, December 3, 1981.
[48] *Ibid.*
[49] *Jerusalem Post*, September 18, 1981.
[50] *New York Times*, December 21, 1981 carried a transcript of Begin's statement.

Chapter 3

[1] *Washington Post*, December 3, 1982, p. A28, quoting a letter to Senator Mark Hatfield (R-Ore.) from Deputy Secretary of State Kenneth W. Dam. For an earlier analysis of the way the Soviet threat was being used against Israel, see *Christian Science Monitor*, February 23, 1982, p. 3.

[2] The monograph series was done under the direction of Steven Rosen who was hired by AIPAC in 1982. Rosen came from the RAND corporation where he had authored the 1981 study, referred to earlier in the paper, urging the U.S. to rely heavily on Israel in order to counter the Soviet threat in the Persian Gulf. After he came to AIPAC, the study was published under the title "The Strategic Value of Israel" and Rosen, as AIPAC's new research director, oversaw publication of the rest of the monograph series.

[3] Haig, *Caveat*, p. 328.

[4] *Ibid.*, p. 329.

[5] Samuel W. Lewis, "The United States and Israel: Constancy and Change," *The Middle East Ten Years After Camp David*, William B. Quandt, ed. (Washington DC: The Brookings Institution, 1988), p. 236.

[6] *IFR*, 1981-82, #105, p. 273.

[7] *Ibid.*, #106, pp. 277-78.

[8] Eytan Gilboa, *American Public Opinion and the Arab-Israeli Conflict* (Lexington Books, 1987), pp. 132-34.

[9] *Ibid.*

[10] *New York Times*, May 13, 1982.

[11] Schiff and Ya'ari, *Israel's Lebanon War*, p. 71.

[12] *Ibid.*, p. 228.

[13] For one important perspective on the administration's view of events in Lebanon, see Caspar Weinberger, *Fighting for Peace* (New York: Warner Books, 1990), p. 152.

[14] *Ibid.*, p. 162.

[15] Lewis, "US and Israel," p. 241.

[16] Haig, *Caveat*, p. 339.

[17] *Ibid.*, p. 334.

[18] Bob Woodward, *Veil: The Secret Wars of the CIA 1981-87* (Simon and Schuster, 1987), p. 217.

[19] Haig, *Caveat*, p. 344.

[20] Schiff and Ya'ari, *Israel's Lebanon War*, p. 221.

[21] *Ibid.*, p. 225.

[22] *IFR*, 1982-84, p. 176.

[23] Gilboa, *Public Opinion*, p. 146.

Chapter 4

[1] Lewis, "US and Israel, p. 241.
[2] *IFR*, 1982-84, p. 244.
[3] *AFP, Current Documents*, 1982, p. 747.
[4] Spiegel, *The Other Conflict*, p. 423.
[5] See Assistant Secretary for Near East Affairs Veliotes' discussion about US support for the rapid deployment force in Jordan on February 2, 1983. *AFP*, 1983, p. 725.
[6] Woodward, *Veil*, p. 245.
[7] *AFP*, 1983, p. 757.
[8] *Ibid.*, 1983, pp. 672-674. It is also interesting to note Shultz' adoption, like Haig before him, of the term "strategic partner" to describe Israel--not asset, but partner.
[9] *Ibid*.
[10] Howard M. Sachar, *A History of Israel*, Volume II (Oxford University Press, 1987), pp. 214-5.
[11] *AFP*, 1983, #276, p. 635 and p. 703.
[12] *Ibid.*, pp. 716-18.
[13] *Ibid.*, #322, p. 715.
[14] Gilboa, *Public Opinion*, p. 147-8.
[15] Hedrick Smith, *The Power Game* (New York: Random House, 1988), pp. 219-231.
[16] *AFP*, 1983, p. 720.
[17] Spiegel, *The Other Conflict*, p. 427.
[18] *Jerusalem Post* International Edition, November 20-26, 1983, p. 1.
[19] Nimrod Novik, *Encounter with Reality: Reagan and the Middle East*, JCSS Study No. 1 (Boulder: Westview Press, 1985), p. 54.
[20] *AFP*, 1983, p. 721.
[21] Background briefing, The White House, Office of the Press Secretary, November 29, 1983.
[22] *New York Times*, December 1, 1983, p. A6.

Chapter 5

[1] Interview with Menachem Meron, December 11, 1990.
[2] See *New York Times*, January 15, 1984.
[3] *Washington Post*, June 21, 1984, p. 1.
[4] For fuller treatment of this relationship, see Dore Gold, *Israel as an American Non-NATO Ally*. Also see Aharon Klieman and Reuven Pedatzur, *Rearming Israel: Defense Procurement Through the 1990s*, JCSS Study no. 17, 1991.
[5] For both Reagan's and Shamir's statements on November 29, 1983 see *AFP*, 1983, pp. 721-722.
[6] White House Backgrounder, November 29, 1983.
[7] *Washington Post*, November 30, 1983, p. A1.
[8] *AFP*, 1983, p. 720.
[9] *New York Times*, January 15, 1984.
[10] Ibid.
[11] Leslie Gelb in *New York Times*, July 20, 1984.
[12] Ibid.
[13] Interview with Marvin Feuerwerger, October 3, 1990.
[14] Interview with Yitzhak Rabin, December 12, 1990.
[15] *Jerusalem Post*, September 13, 1986, p. 1.
[16] *Le Figaro*, August 9, 1990, p. 6. FBIS, NES-90-156, August 13, 1990, p. 59.
[17] Yitzhak Rabin pointed out that capabilities, once developed, could be used, if necessary, even in inter-Arab disputes. Rabin interview, December 12, 1990.
[18] It is important not to underestimate the importance of training and exercises for establishing emergency procedures which could be used in any crisis, regardless of the original training mission. General John Galvin, the Supreme Allied Commander in Europe, emphasized this point, albeit in a different context, in an interview in *Armed Forces Journal International*, April 1991, p. 70. He noted that, in the buildup to the Gulf War, no plan existed for moving the VII Corps out of Germany to Saudi Arabia: "That's 40,000 vehicles, 90,000 people, 600 trains and over 100 ships.... But what we did have was a lot of REFORGERs (Return of Forces to Germany Exercises) behind us. And so all we had to do was say, OK gang, its REFORGER in reverse, Let's Go! And everybody from sergeants on up knew what to do."
[19] *AFP*, 1983, p. 720.
[20] *Jerusalem Post* International Edition, May 27, 1984, p. 1.
[21] *AFP*, 1984, p. 535.
[22] Dershowitz, *The Reagan Administration*, p. 175.
[23] Ibid.
[24] The Washington Institute for Near East Policy, "Chronology of Strategic Cooperation," in *The U.S.-Israeli Relationship: Burdens and Benefits*, The Center for Foreign Policy Options (California, 1988), p. 32.
[25] Ambassador William Brown to the UJA President's Club, August 20, 1990.
[26] *Ha'aretz*, November 4, 1988.

[27] *Washington Institute Chronology*, p. 33.
[28] *Davar*, March 12, 1986, p. 1.
[29] *Washington Institute Chronology*, pp. 33-34.
[30] Dershowitz, *Key Statements*, p. 111.
[31] *Washington Post*, December 1, 1983.
[32] Weinberger, *Fighting for Peace*.
[33] See, for instance, Murphy's testimony on Capitol Hill in both April and October 1986, where he warns that 30 years of balanced US approach to the region, with its attendant capability to mediate between both sides, was in jeopardy. *AFP*, 1986, pp. 362-66 and pp. 368-370.
[34] *Washington Post*, August 5, 1986, p. A1.
[35] *New York Times*, December 22, 1985, p. 1; *Washington Post*, June 15, 1986, p. 1.
[36] *Washington Post*, August 5, 1986, p. 1.
[37] The author visited the memorial at the suggestion of Dr. Hanan Alon, Director of Foreign Affairs, Ministry of Defense, who also supplied the details of the Darby story. The plaque reads: "In memory of R.Admiral Jack N. Darby, USN, An Architect of U.S.-Israeli Strategic Cooperation, and a Friend."
[38] *Washington Post*, August 5, 1986, p. 1.
[39] *Ibid*.
[40] *Ibid*.
[41] *Middle East Military Balance 1988-89*, ed. by Shlomo Gazit, Jaffee Center for Strategic Studies, Tel Aviv University (Boulder: Westview Press, 1990), p. 187.
[42] *Congressional Quarterly Weekly Report*, January 20, 1990, p. 197. For a more complete listing of US-Israeli cooperative projects in this area see Dore Gold, *Parameters*.
[43] *American-Arab Affairs*, Spring, 1987 interview with Richard L. Armitage, p. 36.
[44] Dershowitz, *Key Statements*, p. 117.
[45] *AFP*, 1988, pp. 417-19.
[46] White House Statement, April 21, 1988, *AFP*, 1988, p. 415.

Chapter 6

[1] For examples, see *Washington Post*, December 19, 1989, p. A16; or *Christian Science Monitor*, December 12, 1989, p. 5; or see Martin Indyk's comments, reported by *Jerusalem Post* International Edition, week ending December 9, 1989, p. 5, where he stated that the changing strategic environment "cannot but diminish Israel's importance over time... There will be a step-by-step dismantling of some parts of the strategic structure."

[2] One of the few efforts to actually analyze the potential effects on Israel of changes occurring in the US defense establishment was by Dr. Dore Gold, *Jerusalem Post*, January 19, 1990.

[3] See *USIS Press Clips*, March 13, 1990, pp. 56-60; see also Cheney's speech to the Anti-Defamation League of B'nai B'rith, June 15, 1990, found in *ADL Bulletin*, September 1990, pp. 6-7.

[4] Under Secretary of Defense Paul Wolfowitz, *USIS Press Clips*, NXE 309, December 19, 1990, p. 106.

[5] Jerusalem Domestic Service in English, September 11, 1989, FBIS NES-89-174, September 11, 1989, p. 23.

[6] *Washington Post*, September 27, 1990, p. A44.

[7] *Ha'aretz*, September 24, 1990, p. A1.

[8] Of course, from the perspective of Israeli defense industries, there is also a negative aspect to storing American weaponry and equipment: if the IDF can count on US equipment, it will not buy it from domestic Israeli industry.

[9] See either the speeches of Begin and Sharon in the early 1980s or see Rosen, "The Strategic Value of Israel."

[10] *Jerusalem Post*, September 10-11, 1989.

[11] State Department Briefing Paper, January 19, 1990, United States Information Service, Tel Aviv. Also see *Jerusalem Post*, January 19, 1990, p. 1.

[12] *Jerusalem Post*, March 11, 1990, p. 1.

[13] Parallel talks were also proceeding with Saudi Arabia and the UAE regarding the sale of the system to them.

[14] *Jerusalem Post* International Edition, September 2, 1989, p. 4.

[15] Cheney's March 13, 1990 UJA speech.

[16] *Ma'ariv*, March, 30, 1990.

[17] For text of the May 22, 1989 AIPAC speech, see United States Department of State, Bureau of Public Affairs, Current Policy No. 1176.

[18] See *Jerusalem Post*, May 11, 1990, p. 6.

[19] For the text of his public proposal, see *International Herald Tribune*, January 17, 1990, p. 6.

[20] *Jerusalem Report*, June 20, 1991, p. 37.

Chapter 7

[1] See, for example, *International Herald Tribune*, August 6, 1990, p. 6. See also an interview with Yuval Ne'eman on August 9, 1990 (Jerusalem Domestic Service in English); *Ma'ariv*, August 6, 1990, p. A1, quoting unnamed senior Israeli defense official; and *Ma'ariv*, August 8, 1990 quoting Ariel Sharon.

[2] Zeev Schiff commentary, *Ha'aretz*, October 5, 1990. Bob Woodward also highlights how uncertain Washington was in those initial days whether King Fahd, the Saudi ruler, would even allow the US to protect Saudi Arabia. Bob Woodward, *The Commanders* (Simon & Schuster, 1991), pp. 239-273.

[3] *New York Times*, August 15, 1990, p. 2, citing administration sources.

[4] Ibid. Tom Friedman noted that the only two Middle Eastern leaders not telephoned by Bush after the Gulf crisis began were Saddam Hussein and Yitzhak Shamir.

[5] State Department Fact Sheet, March 1, 1991, reprinted in *USIS Press Clips*, March 25, 1991, p. 21.

[6] Reprinted in *Washington Post*, August 16, 1990, p. A25.

[7] *Jerusalem Post*, August 12, 1990, p. 2.

[8] Ibid., October 17, 1990, p. 7, quoting Dr. Mustafa Khalil. This theme was echoed in the author's interviews in January 1991, in Egypt, with Ambassador Salah Bassiouny and Dr. Ali E. Hillal Dessouki.

[9] In fact, opinion was split within Israel over whether to push for debt forgiveness due to the adverse effect such a course would have on Israel's international credit standing.

[10] *Time*, November 5, 1990, p. 44.

[11] IDF Radio in Hebrew, August 14, 1990. FBIS-NES-90-158, August 15, 1990, p. 30.

[12] *Jerusalem Television* in Hebrew, August 10, 1990. FBIS-NES-90-155, August 10, 1990, p. 52.

[13] Indeed, several Israeli experts in and out of government suggested during interviews conducted before the war that I wait and see what would happen in the event hostilities occurred--implying that at that point, the US would be much more willing to rely on Israel's military prowess.

[14] *Washington Post*, November 13, 1990, p. B1.

[15] *Ha'aretz*, October 5, 1990.

[16] Baker testimony to House Foreign Affairs Committee, October 18, 1990, *USIS Press Clips*, October 18, 1990, pp. 120-21.

[17] See *Wall Street Journal*, October 23, 1990, p. A-13 and *Jerusalem Post*, October 31, 1990, p. 10.

[18] *Jerusalem Post*, August 31, 1990, p. 1.

[19] Both men were asked about the possibility of military action involving Israel and the U.S. Michel opined that the U.S. had helped Israel build up its forces "to defend itself in just such a situation," whereas Dole responded that he "would not expect any role by Israel unless it were attacked." *MacNeil-Lehrer Newshour*, August 3, 1990.

[20] *New York Times*, September 28, 1990, p. 1.
[21] *Jerusalem Post*, September 28, 1990, p. 1.
[22] For example, see Baker's testimony to the House Foreign Affairs Committee, October 18, 1990.
[23] *Jerusalem Post*, September 30, 1990, p. 1.
[24] *Ibid.*, September 28, 1990, p. 1.
[25] *Ibid.*, October 26, 1990, p. 3.
[26] See *USIS Press Clips*, October 25, 1990, p. 126.
[27] For instance, see Secretary Cheney's remarks before the Senate Armed Services Committee on December 3, 1990 (*Department of State Bulletin*, Jan-April 1991, pp. 34-36) and President Bush's Press Conference on November 8, 1990 (same *DOS Bulletin*, p. 7).
[28] *Yediot Aharonot*, December 6, 1990.
[29] *Washington Post*, November 8, 1990; See also Lally Weymouth's article in *Washington Post* on November 13, 1990, p. B1.
[30] *Ha'aretz*, October 5, 1990.
[31] *Washington Post*, November 8, 1990.
[32] *Ha'aretz*, November 7, 1990.
[33] Weymouth, *Washington Post*, November 13, 1990.
[34] *Washington Post*, January 2, 1991, p. A17.
[35] *New York Times*, reprinted in *International Herald Tribune*, March 5, 1991, p. 5.
[36] *Ibid.*

Chapter 8

[1] For one of the fullest accounts of the Patriot story, see *Jerusalem Report*, February 1, 1991, p. 5.
[2] For accounts of the Eagleburger mission see *Jerusalem Post*, January 13, 1991, p. 1, and January 14, 1991, p. 1; Also, *International Herald Tribune*, January 14, 1991, p. 1.
[3] Bob Woodward, however, claims that Israel accepted the offer at this time. *Commanders*, p. 363.
[4] *Jerusalem Post*, January 14, 1991.
[5] *International Herald Tribune*, January 16, 1991, p. 3.
[6] Ibid.
[7] Ibid.
[8] *Jerusalem Post*, January 23, 1991, p. 1.
[9] Woodward, *Commanders*, p. 364.
[10] *Jerusalem Post*, January 15, 1991, p. 1.
[11] Woodward, *Commanders*, p. 363.
[12] Ibid., p. 370.
[13] *Jerusalem Post*, January 17, 1991, p. 1.
[14] Most of this initial accounting of events is taken from a retrospective report pulled together by *Washington Post* on March 19, 1991.
[15] *New York Times*, March 6, 1991.
[16] *Washington Post*, March 19, 1991.
[17] Pentagon sources reported that, early in the air war, 15 percent of CENTCOM's air assets were diverted to searching for the Scuds, which were, from the military's point of a view, militarily-worthless targets. *Newsweek*, March 18, 1991, p. 24.
[18] *International Herald Tribune*, January 16, 1991, p. 1.
[19] *Jerusalem Report*, January 31, 1991, p. 10.
[20] *Jerusalem Post*, January 21, 1991, p. 1.
[21] April 8, 1991 interview with David Frost.
[22] *Jerusalem Post*, January 29, 1991, p. 1.
[23] Cheney speech to meeting of Jewish leaders March 5, 1991, *USIS Press Clips*, March 6, 1991, p. 31.
[24] *Aviation Week and Space Technology*, January 28, 1991, p. 19.
[25] Interview with Major General Avihu Bin-Nun, *Yediot Aharonot*, February 1, 1991.
[26] *Jerusalem Report*, March 7, 1991, p. 12. See also *Aviation Week and Space Technology*, February 4, 1991, p. 24.
[27] Rabin interview, December 12, 1990.
[28] Shamir interview in *Yediot Aharonot*, FBIS-NES-90-235, December 6, 1990, p. 27.
[29] *Al Hamishmar*, February 1, 1991, p. 7.
[30] *International Herald Tribune*, February 21, 1991, p. 2.
[31] Defense Secretary Cheney commented in a Q&A session after a speech to the Washington Institute for Near East Policy on April 29, 1991: "I cannot say that the coalition would have broken up if the Israelis had gotten involved, but I'm glad we never had to test that proposition." *USIS Press Clips*, April 29, 1991, p. 96.

Chapter 9

[1] Powell remarks to AIPAC, March 19, 1991, *USIS Press Clips*, March 19, 1991, NXE 203, p. 75.
[2] Cheney before Jewish leaders, March 6, 1991, *USIS Press Clips*, March 6, 1991, NEA 313, p. 30.
[3] *Ibid*.
[4] *International Herald Tribune*, June 1-2, 1991, p. 1; also *Jerusalem Report*, June 6, 1991, p. 6.
[5] Interview with Dr. William Quandt, October 30, 1990.
[6] Bush-Mitterrand press conference, March 14, 1991, *USIS Press Clips*, p. 40.
[7] POMCUS stocks are depots of military equipment for large-size units kept in storage in the region for later US use.
[8] Interview with Colonel James Carney, Defense Attache at the American Embassy, Tel Aviv, Israel, June 5, 1991.
[9] *Ibid*.
[10] See Klieman and Pedatzur, *Rearming Israel*, p. 304.
[11] See Gold, *Israel as an American Non-NATO Ally*, pp. 95-96.
[12] *Washington Post*, July 24, 1991, p. A4.
[13] Powell remarks to AIPAC, March 19, 1991.
[14] See the aforementioned Powell and Cheney speeches. Also see testimony by Arthur H. Hughes, deputy assistant secretary of defense for Near East and South Asian Affairs, before the House Subcommittee on Europe and the Middle East, March 6, 1991; *USIS Press Clips*, March 6, 1991, NXE 307, pp. 84-86.
[15] Tom Friedman, *New York Times*, March 17, 1991, p. C1.
[16] For a transcript of the Eagleburger press conference, see USIA, *The Wireless File*, January 21, 1991, p. 13.
[17] Interview with Marvin Feuerwerger, October 3, 1990.
[18] Interview with Dr. William Quandt, October 30, 1990.
[19] Interview with Hanan Bar-On, former deputy director general of the Israel Ministry of Foreign Affairs, February 4, 1991.
[20] Zeev Schiff, "Israel After the War," *Foreign Affairs*, Spring 1991, pp 19-21.
[21] Interview with Ambassador William Brown, October 30, 1990.

Appendix 1

MEMORANDUM OF UNDERSTANDING BETWEEN THE GOVERNMENT OF THE UNITED STATES AND THE GOVERNMENT OF ISRAEL ON STRATEGIC COOPERATION
30 November 1981

PREAMBLE

This memorandum of understanding reaffirms the common bonds of friendship between the United States and Israel and builds on the mutual security relationship that exists between the two nations. The parties recognize the need to enhance strategic cooperation to deter all threats from the Soviet Union to the region. Noting the longstanding and fruitful cooperation for mutual security that has developed between the two countries, the parties have decided to establish a framework for continued consultation and cooperation to enhance their national security by deterring such threats to the whole region.

The parties have reached the following agreements in order to achieve the above aims.

ARTICLE I

United States-Israel strategic cooperation, as set forth in this memorandum, is designed against the threat to peace and security of the region caused by the Soviet Union or Soviet-controlled forces from outside the region introduced into the region. It has the following broad purposes:

A. To enable the parties to act cooperatively and in a timely manner to deal with the above-mentioned threat.

B. To provide each other with military assistance for operations of their forces in the area that may be required to cope with this threat.

C. The strategic cooperation between the parties is not directed at any state or group of states within the region. It is intended solely for defensive purposes against the above-mentioned threat.

ARTICLE II

1. The fields in which strategic cooperation will be carried out to prevent the above-mentioned threat from endangering the security of the region include:

    A. Military cooperation between the parties, as may be agreed by the parties.

    B. Joint military exercises, including naval and air exercises in the Eastern Mediterranean sea, as agreed upon by the parties.

    C. Cooperation for the establishment and maintenance of joint readiness activities, as agreed upon by the parties.

    D. Other areas within the basic scope and purpose of this agreement, as may be jointly agreed.

2. Details of activities within these fields of cooperation shall be worked out by the parties in accordance with the provisions of Article III below. The cooperation will include, as appropriate, planning, preparations, and exercises.

ARTICLE III

1. The Secretary of Defense and the Minister of Defense shall establish a coordinating council to further the purposes of this memorandum.

    A. To coordinate and provide guidance to joint working groups.

    B. To monitor the implementation of cooperation in the fields agreed upon by the parties within the scope of this agreement.

    C. To hold periodic meetings, in Israel and the United States, for the purposes of discussing and resolving outstanding issues and to further the objectives set forth in this memorandum. Special meetings can be held at the request of either party. The Secretary of Defense and Minister of Defense will chair these meetings whenever possible.

2. Joint working groups will address the following issues:

    A. Military Cooperation between the parties, including joint U.S.-Israel exercises in the Eastern Mediterranean sea.

    B. Cooperation for the establishment of joint readiness activities including access to maintenance facilities and other infrastructure, consistent with the basic purposes of this agreement.

    C. Cooperation in research and development, building on past cooperation in this area.

D. Cooperation in defense trade.

E. Other fields within the basic scope and purpose of this agreement, such as questions of prepositioning, as agreed by the coordinating council.

3. The future agenda for the work of the joint working groups, their composition and procedures for reporting to the coordinating council shall be agreed upon by the parties.

ARTICLE IV

This memorandum shall enter into force upon exchange of notification that required procedures have been completed by each party. If either party considers it necessary to terminate this memorandum of understanding, it may do so by notifying the other party six months in advance of the effective date of termination.

ARTICLE V

Nothing in this memorandum shall be considered as derogating from previous agreements and understandings between the parties.

ARTICLE VI

The parties share the understanding that nothing in this memorandum is intended or shall in any way prejudge the rights and obligations which devolve or may devolve upon either government under the charter of the United Nations or under international law. The parties reaffirm their faith in the purposes and principles of the charter of the United Nations and their aspiration to live in peace with all countries in the region.

Appendix 2

MEMORANDUM OF AGREEMENT BETWEEN THE UNITED STATES OF AMERICA AND THE STATE OF ISRAEL REGARDING JOINT POLITICAL, SECURITY AND ECONOMIC COOPERATION

PREAMBLE

The parties to this Memorandum of Agreement reaffirm the close relationship between the United States of America and Israel, based upon common goals, interests, and values; welcome the achievements made in strategic, economic, industrial, and technological cooperation; recognize the mutual benefits of the United States-Israel Free Trade Agreement; take note of United States economic and security assistance to Israel; and note that Israel is currently designated, for the purposes of Section 1105 of the 1987 National Defense Authorization Act, as a major non-NATO ally of the United States. The parties wish to enhance their relationship through the establishment of a comprehensive framework for continued consultation and cooperation and have reached the following agreements in order to achieve this aim.

ARTICLE I

The United States and Israel recognize the value of their unique dialogue and agree to continue frequent consultations and periodic meetings between the President and the Prime Minister, between the Secretary of State and the Minister of Foreign Affairs, between the Secretary of Defense and the Minister of Defense, and between other Cabinet-level officials. In these meetings, international and bilateral issues of immediate and significant concern to both countries will be discussed as appropriate.

ARTICLE II

A. The Director General of the Ministry of Foreign Affairs and the Under Secretary of State for Political Affairs will meet regularly, for a Joint Political Consultation (JPC) to discuss a wide range of international issues of mutual interest with a view toward increasing their mutual understanding and appreciation of these issues.

B. The United States Agency for International Development and Israel's Ministry of Foreign Affairs, Division of International Cooperation (Mashav) meet periodically to coordinate and facilitate, as appropriate, programs of cooperative assistance to developing countries.

ARTICLE III

The United States and Israel reaffirm the importance of the following U.S.-Israeli Joint Groups:

A. The Joint Political Military Group (JPMG) is the forum in which the two states discuss and implement, pursuant to existing arrangements, joint cooperative efforts such as combined planning, joint exercises, and logistics. The JPMG also discusses current political-military issues of mutual strategic concern.

1. The JPMG is a binational, interagency group co-chaired by the Director General of the Israeli Ministry of Defense and the U.S. Assistant Secretary of State for Politico-Military Affairs.

2. The JPMG normally meets biannually, alternating between Israel and the United States.

B. The Joint Security Assistance Planning Group (JSAP) is the forum in which the two states review Israel's requests for security assistance in light of current threat assessments and U.S. budgetary capabilities and agree upon proposed levels of security assistance. The JSAP also discusses issues related to security assistance, such as industrial and technological cooperation, as well as issues related to Israel's inclusion among those countries currently designated as major non-NATO allies of the United States for the purpose of cooperative research and development under Section 1105 of the 1987 National Defense Authorization Act.

1. The JSAP is a binational, interagency group co-chaired by the Director General of the Ministry of Defense and the Under Secretary of State for Security Assistance, Science, and Technology.

2. The JSAP currently meets annually, in Washington, D.C.

C. The Joint Economic Development Group (JEDG) is the forum which discusses developments in Israel's economy. With a view to stimulating economic growth and self-reliance, the JEDG exchanges views on Israeli economic policy planning, stabilization efforts, and structural reform. The JEDG also evaluates Israel's requests for U.S. economic assistance.

1. The JEDG is a binational, interagency group co-chaired by the Director General of the Ministry of Finance and the Under Secretary of State for Economic Affairs. The group includes private U.S. and Israeli economists invited by their respective countries.

2. The JEDG currently meets biannually, alternating between the United States and Israel.

ARTICLE IV

This Memorandum of Agreement does not derogate from any existing agreements or undertakings between the two states nor in any way prejudices the rights and obligations of either state under the Charter of the United Nations or under international law. In accordance with the above, the parties reaffirm their aspirations to live in peace with all countries. This agreement shall come into effect upon signature, shall be valid for an initial period of five years, and shall thereafter be renewed for additional periods of five years unless either party notifies the other prior to the expiration of a five year period that it wishes to terminate the agreement.

DONE at Washington and Jerusalem, in duplicate, in the English language, the twenty-first day of April, 1988, the fourth day of Iyar, 5748, and the   day of April, 1988, the   day of Iyar, 5748.

About the Author

Karen L. Puschel has been a Soviet affairs specialist with the US Department of State since 1981. While on leave of absence, she wrote this study as a guest scholar at the Jaffee Center for Strategic Studies, under funding from the US Institute of Peace. In 1988, Ms. Puschel was an International Affairs Fellow at the Council on Foreign Relations in New York. Her past publications include "Can Moscow live with SDI" (*Survival*, January 1989) and "Soviet Aerospace: Reading for the Future" (*National Defense*, June 1990). In the summer of 1992 she will take up a position at the US Embassy in Moscow.

JCSS Publications

JCSS Publications present the findings and assessments of the Center's research staff. Each paper represents the work of a single investigator or a team. Such teams may also include research fellows who are not members of the Center's staff. Views expressed in the Center's publications are those of the authors and do not necessarily reflect the views of the Center, its trustees, officers, or other staff members or the organizations and individuals that support its research. Thus the publication of a work by JCSS signifies that it is deemed worthy of public consideration but does not imply endorsement of conclusions or recommendations.

Editor
Aharon Yariv

Executive Editor
Joseph Alpher

Editorial Board

Mordechai Abir
Yehezkel Dror
Saul Friedlander
Shlomo Gazit
Mordechai Gur
Yehoshafat Harkabi
Walter Laqueur

Yuval Ne'eman
Yitzhak Rabin
Aryeh Shalev
Israel Tal
Saadia Touval
David Vital

The Jaffee Center for Strategic Studies Recent Publications in English

1991-1992 Subscription Series
Study no. 18 Mark A. Heller, *The Dynamics of Soviet Policy in the Middle East: Between Old Thinking and New.*
Study no. 19 Dore Gold, *Israel as an American Non-NATO Ally: Parameters of Defense-Industrial Cooperation.*
Study no. 20 Karen L. Puschel, *US-Israeli Strategic Cooperation in the Post-Cold War Era: An American Perspective.*

War in the Gulf: Implications for Israel
    Report of a JCSS Study Group. Edited by Joseph Alpher.
The Middle East Military Balance 1990-1991
    Edited by Shlomo Gazit; with Zeev Eytan.

1990 Subscription Series
Study no. 15 Dore Gold, ed., *Arms Control in the Middle East.*
Study no. 16 Aryeh Shalev, *The Intifada: Causes and Effects.*
Study no. 17 Aharon Klieman and Reuven Pedatzur, *Rearming Israel: Defense Procurement Through the 1990s.*

Books
Anat Kurz, ed., *Contemporary Trends in World Terrorism*
    (New York: Praeger/Greenwood, 1987).
Ephraim Kam, *Surprise Attack: The Victim's Perspective*
    (Cambridge: Harvard University Press, 1988).
Efraim Karsh, ed., *The Iran-Iraq War: Impact and Implications*
    (London: Macmillan, 1989).
The West Bank and Gaza: Israel's Options for Peace
and
Israel, the West Bank and Gaza: Toward a Solution
Reports of JCSS Study Groups. Coordinator: Joseph Alpher, 1989.